The PRACTICAL GUIDE to RTI

SIX STEPS TO SCHOOL-WIDE SUCCESS

REBECCA JOHNSON · VICKI WEATHERMAN

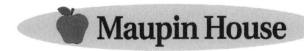

Maupin House

The Practical Guide to RTI
Six Steps to School-wide Success
By Rebecca Johnson & Vicki Weatherman

Cover Design: Studio Montage
Book Design and Composition: Rick Soldin

Library of Congress Cataloging-in-Publication Data

Johnson, Rebecca, (Rebecca A.), 1966-
  The practical guide to RTI : six steps to school-wide success / by Rebecca Johnson and Vicki Weatherman.
        p. cm.
  Includes bibliographical references.
  ISBN-13: 978-1-936700-56-1
  ISBN-10: 1-936700-56-5
1. Response to intervention (Learning disabled children)—Handbooks, manuals, etc. 2. Learning disabled
children—Education—Handbooks, manuals, etc. I. Weatherman, Vicki, 1958- II. Title.
  LC4705.J66 2013
  371.9—dc23

                                                                                          2012021134

Maupin House publishes professional resources for K-12 educators. Contact us for tailored, in-house training or to schedule an author for a workshop or conference. Visit **www.maupinhouse.com** to browse our other titles and download free lesson plans.

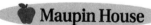 **Maupin House**

Maupin House Publishing, Inc.
2300 NW 71st Place
Gainesville, FL 32653
www.maupinhouse .com
Phone: 800-524-0634
Fax: 352-373-5546
info@maupinhouse.com

10 9 8 7 6 5 4 3 2 1

Acknowledgments and Dedication

We would like to acknowledge the people whose hard work and dedication help make this work possible.

We gratefully acknowledge our school psychologists, who from the very beginning, guided us through the process with enthusiasm and helped make the transition from the discrepancy model to the RTI model seamless, natural, and easy. We had three different psychologists throughout these years, and each helped us grow in his or her own unique way.

We applaud our teachers who embraced the many changes that continued to increase our students' chances for success. They trusted the process and knew that if we stayed the course, the benefits would outweigh any obstacles.

We cannot forget our invaluable paraprofessionals who are truly the anchor for our program. Their enthusiasm when working with students, willingness to master all interventions, and dedication, integrity, and patience are truly some of the reasons RTI has been so successful at our school.

Finally, we would like to acknowledge our students. Students come to us eagerly wanting to learn. We appreciate and applaud their effort, flexibility, and desire to learn. Thank you for your all-star attitudes!

This book is dedicated to each of these individuals and groups. Without their support and hard work, it would never have become a reality.

Contents

Introduction

Our combined forty years of public school experience have all been in the fifth largest school district in the United States: the Clark County School District (CCSD) in Nevada. During that time, we have watched the evolution of assistance to struggling students, and we have helped lead our school to integrate RTI successfully school-wide.

Like many other districts, the CCSD once used a team Problem-Solving Model known as the Student Intervention Team (SIT) or Student Intervention Process (SIP). The team consisted of a random number of teachers and/or administrators who met on a regular basis to "monitor student progress." We use the phrase "monitor student progress" loosely because, in many cases, the process did not actually monitor anything.

Traditionally, what happened at these team meetings was quite the opposite of progress monitoring. A teacher would fill out an enormous packet of information about a failing student and request an appearance at one of the team meetings. Because so many students would fall into the failing category, a teacher could wait several weeks before getting scheduled to present information on a student. If the teacher came to the meeting prepared, she would share the student's work samples, assessment results, and strategies that had been implemented to help the student make progress. The team would listen to the teacher and then provide one of two sets of advice.

Many times, the teacher would be sent away with additional ideas for interventions that should be tried and then scheduled for a date to return to the team a few weeks later to discuss the results. If the teacher had provided the team with enough evidence of instruction and support, however, the team would recommend that the student be referred to a Multidisciplinary Team (MDT). The MDT would review all the same information and would again determine if the teacher had exhausted all possible options to provide the student with adequate instruction.

Once *again*, the teacher could be sent back to try more interventions on her own. If the teacher was lucky, the MDT would recommend assessing the student to determine if the child was eligible for special-education services under the Individuals with Disabilities Education Act (IDEA).

In the meantime, the calendar year would pass at an alarming rate, and the student would continue to fail while awaiting the outcome of the assessments. The entire process of referring a student for assistance could take an academic school year or longer. Many teachers experienced severe frustration with this process and, at times, simply refused to participate in it at all. The traditional process was set up as a lose-lose for everyone.

Enter RTI

At the end of the 2002-2003 school year, our director of psychological services asked the school to pilot a new process for helping struggling students called Response to Intervention (RTI).

Luckily, we had already created a strong Professional Learning Community (PLC) in which the teachers collaborated regularly on instructional strategies and crafted common expectations and common assessments (Dufour and Eaker, 1998).

At this time, IDEA was in the process of being reauthorized, recommending documentation of a child's response to research-based interventions as part of the evaluation procedure. As a result of the IDEA reauthorization process, the newly assigned psychologist was very excited to implement RTI, and we began experimenting with the process.

Initially, the only change we made was to begin pencil-and-paper tracking of student progress in some basic skills. During the next eight years, we experimented with our procedures, and the process transformed into something nobody could have predicted.

During that time, we dramatically reduced the number of students who were referred for special-education testing. Eventually, 100 percent of the students we referred qualified for special-education services.

The best outcome was that we increased our overall student achievement on state proficiency tests by more than twenty percentage points in English/language arts and more than thirty-five percentage points in math. (Figure 1 shows proficiency growth throughout the seven years of implementation.)

We were invited to present our findings at various conferences and schools throughout Nevada. Because the requests continued, we decided to create this resource to guide principals and teachers through the step-by-step process as they implemented RTI at the building level.

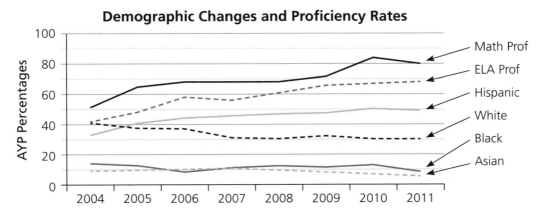

Figure 1: Demographic Changes and Proficiency Rates

What You Will Find in This Resource

This book compiles all the fine-tuning we have done on the RTI process since 2003. It is still a work in progress. Although we have data that supports our success with RTI, at heart, we are practitioners writing this book for other practitioners who simply want to know where to start and how to sustain RTI in a practical and effective way.

> This book is for practitioners who simply want to know where to start and how to sustain RTI in a practical and effective way.

It is important to note that the six steps flow together so smoothly that it is often difficult to separate them completely. We have attempted to separate them for teaching purposes and then illustrate how the steps work together in three case studies.

Chapter One begins with a discussion of tiered instruction. Chapter Two reviews the institutional underpinning required for RTI success: a collaborative, problem-solving culture and a team that is able to plan and/or support the RTI process and tiered instruction.

> It is important to note that the six steps flow together so smoothly that it is often difficult to separate them completely.

The next six chapters take you through six steps for implementing a three-tiered RTI intervention process. Chapters Three and Four lead you through identifying and diagnosing the exact skill deficiencies of students who struggle with Tier 1 instruction. Chapter Five provides tips to plan interventions—e.g., how to set achievable goals, identify an acceptable threshold for success, and determine the interventions necessary to achieve the goal.

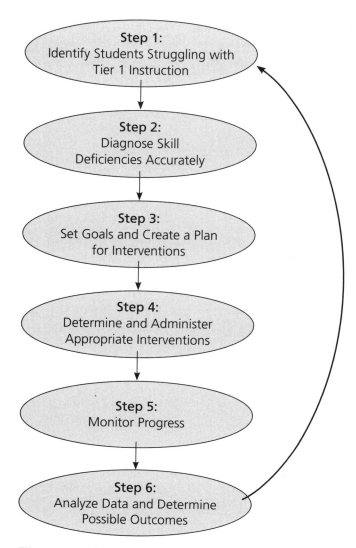

Figure 2: Six Steps to School-wide Success

In Chapters Six and Seven, we will share ideas for implementing interventions and discuss how to monitor progress. Chapter Eight highlights possible outcomes and explains how to plan for your next steps.

The case studies in Chapter Nine follow the journeys of three students: a first-grade ELL student from Mexico, a fourth-grade ELL student who had been retained at his previous school but made rapid gains at our school, and a student who, beginning in the first grade, moved through tier levels for multiple years before being referred to special-education status.

You will find additional sources for RTI information and assessments in the Appendix as well as directions to digitally download all the charts in the book and templates to use at your school.

What You Will Not Find in This Resource

We do not focus on the details of *establishing* a school-wide community that supports RTI. Many resources have been written on this topic, and because the foundation for a school's learning-ready community begins with the principal, this resource assumes that the school has already created the fertile foundation on which a successful RTI program may flourish.

This resource also is not about how to implement high-quality, comprehensive Tier 1 instruction, which is really the first and best way to ensure all students perform at grade-level expectations.

Instead, we focus on what to do for those students for whom Tier 1 is not enough to ensure their successful achievement at grade-level expectations.

Our goal is to guide a school through the RTI implementation process from start to finish. We do not, however, elaborate on the eligibility process for special-education services, but we take you to the point just before the evaluation for determination.

One more disclaimer is that we only have personal experience using these procedures in an elementary school setting. However, many of the procedures presented are the same for secondary schools, and we provide some suggestions for applying them at that level.

This book includes a free digital download of blank templates to use at your school. For directions, turn to the Appendix (p. 93).

We hope this resource will demystify the RTI process and help your school embed RTI as a school-wide culture that supports each student's academic journey.

TIERED INSTRUCTION

In 2004, the reauthorization of the Individuals with Disabilities Education Improvement Act (IDEIA) removed the requirement of the discrepancy model for special-education eligibility determination. Instead, it made recommendations for Response to Intervention (RTI), which documents how a child responds to research-based interventions as part of the evaluation procedure.

At about the same time, the University of Texas at Austin published, "The 3-Tier Reading Model: Reducing Reading Difficulties for Kindergarten Through Third Grade Students." The three-tier instruction/intervention model was emerging as a recommended way to provide support to students with reading difficulties. This instruction/intervention model forms the basis for most of the implementation recommendations in this resource.

Although researchers and practitioners who use a three-tier intervention model define the tiers differently, all versions share similarities. Our experiences implementing RTI have led us to recommend the following tier definitions:

- **Tier 1:** High-quality differentiated instruction for all students
- **Tier 2:** Supplemental small-group interventions for fifteen to thirty minutes per day *in addition* to Tier 1
- **Tier 3:** Intensive, prescriptive interventions *in addition to* Tier 1 and Tier 2, with time variations depending on the diagnosed deficiencies

> Note that a student may need multiple levels of tiered instruction. Students will also move from level to level during the course of a year (or their academic careers).

Figure 3, on the next page, shows the approximate breakdown of the three tiers with the instructional intent for each tier.

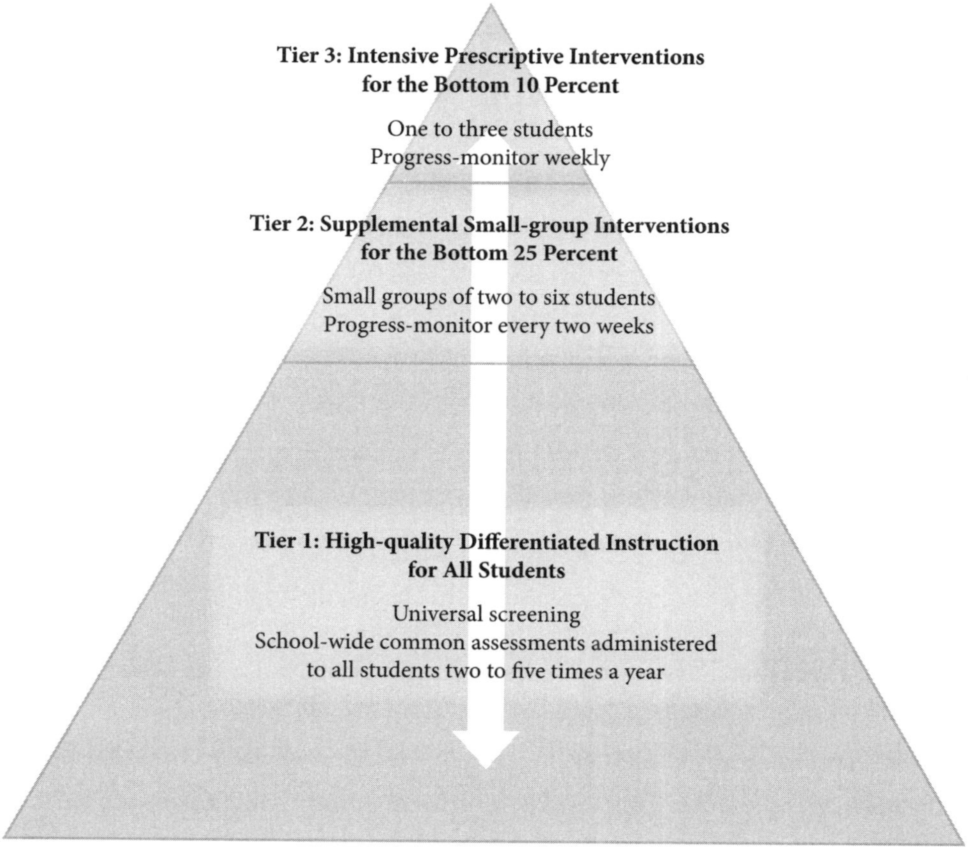

**Tier 3: Intensive Prescriptive Interventions
for the Bottom 10 Percent**

One to three students
Progress-monitor weekly

**Tier 2: Supplemental Small-group Interventions
for the Bottom 25 Percent**

Small groups of two to six students
Progress-monitor every two weeks

**Tier 1: High-quality Differentiated Instruction
for All Students**

Universal screening
School-wide common assessments administered
to all students two to five times a year

Figure 3: The Tiers of Instruction

Tier 1: Core Instruction

The intent of the RTI multi-tiered instruction/intervention process is for all students to achieve proficiency on grade-level standards and be successful at Tier 1. Ensuring high quality, differentiated core instruction for all students is the best way to achieve this lofty goal. After all, a school could spend years creating interventions for students at the Tier 2 and Tier 3 levels with the goal of getting them back to Tier 1. But if Tier 1 is not effective, the students will never catch up.

With this important point made, this book is not about how to implement comprehensive Tier 1 instruction. As stated previously, numerous publications can help you strengthen your Tier 1 instruction in all the individual content areas. Our focus is on what to do for those students for whom Tier 1 is not enough for their successful achievement at grade-level expectations.

We are all aware that many students come to us unprepared to succeed at the Tier 1 level. Schools are working against the effects of poverty, challenges of second-language acquisition, and the apathy of some students and parents. Some students have attendance problems, move from school to school, or suffer from the effects of poor instruction. It is essential that schools have procedures in place to help those students who are not successful in Tier 1.

Identifying struggling learners who require additional intervention—Step 1—takes place during Tier 1 instruction and is discussed in Chapter Three. We will discuss the data sources that are available and make recommendations for analyzing the data and creating Watch Lists of students who may need interventions.

Unfortunately, 20–25 percent of students require additional support outside of Tier 1 to be successful. Therefore, Tier 2 and Tier 3 interventions need to be developed and implemented in an efficient, effective manner.

Tier 2: Supplemental Intervention

RTI research and publications vary a great deal on their recommendations for Tier 2 and Tier 3 interventions. Some even add an additional Tier 4, taking readers through the special-education referral process. Schools and districts have to make adjustments based on the time and resources available to them when determining the logistics of implementing the various options. Regardless of how the next levels are delineated, Tier 2 and Tier 3 interventions must be available to all students who need them.

There is a general consensus among RTI publications that Tier 2 interventions should be conducted in small groups of three to six students, but the recommended frequency and length of the interventions vary. Most researchers indicate the highest success when Tier 2 interventions are implemented three to five times a week for approximately twenty to thirty minutes each time.

> For any intervention model to be successful, Tier 2 and Tier 3 must be implemented in addition to Tier 1 and not as a replacement to regular grade-level instruction.

The greatest recommendation variations are in location, personnel, and the frequency of monitoring intervention progress. Tier 2 can take place during *or* outside of the regular school day as long as the fidelity of the implementation is ensured.

Our teachers implement Tier 2 interventions during a daily scheduled intervention block. Some additional Tier 2 interventions take place during our before- or after-school tutoring sessions. Administrative observations of the intervention block and attendance rosters from the tutoring sessions ensure the fidelity of implementation. The effectiveness of the interventions is determined by progress-monitoring assessments every two weeks.

Tier 3: Intensive Interventions

Students who are unsuccessful in Tier 1 and Tier 2 may require Tier 3 intensive interventions. Our recommendations differ from some traditional models in that we provide Tier 3 interventions in addition to *both* Tier 1 and Tier 2. During our first few years implementing RTI, we struggled with students transferring skills from Tier 3 to Tier 1. Due to this transfer difficulty, we worked to strengthen the Tier 2 portion of the process and provide a scaffolding of skills from Tier 3, through Tier 2, and back into Tier 1. This offers more support for the learners to bridge the gap between the skills they are working on in Tier 3 and application into the Tier 1 curriculum.

As with Tier 2 interventions, Tier 3 interventions should take place a minimum of three to five times a week. They should take place during the school day to monitor the fidelity of implementation and to ensure the intervention is targeting the area(s) of need.

The important criteria to establish here are that students should be able to move fluidly between the tiers as they progress on or struggle with new standards, and they should have access to the interventions as long as they need them and are making growth.

In addition, Tier 3 interventions should be given individually (one on one) if possible, or in a small group (no larger than three students to one teacher). Progress monitoring of the Tier 3 interventions should take place once a week. The differences between Tier 2 and Tier 3—how long the interventions need to take place and how to make adjustments among them—will be discussed more fully in Chapters Five and Six.

CREATE A TEAM FOR RTI SUCCESS

In a random group of educators, you can usually find someone who will say, "*That* will never work at *my* school." We hear this from teachers and psychologists frequently when speaking to them about RTI. Unfortunately, they are correct. Unless you have the right culture within the school, Response to Intervention is not something that can be *tried* to see if it will *work*. A true RTI framework is a school-wide structure and a way to do business.

In their 1998 book, *Professional Learning Communities at Work: Best Practices for Enhancing Student Achievement,* Richard Dufour and Robert Eaker describe how a team of professionals working together can accomplish more than an individual working alone. Our entire intervention model is based on the three critical questions from their book:

- Exactly what is it we want all students to learn?
- How will we know when each student has acquired the essential knowledge and skills?
- What happens in our school when a student does not learn?

Specifically, RTI is the answer to the last question.

RTI implementation assumes, and begins with, a school-wide culture that honors collaboration and problem solving. Your team grows out of that culture and works together through the entire RTI process.

We developed our successful RTI process through a collaborative problem-solving team philosophy. A well-functioning team is fundamental to RTI success because it combines expertise and knowledge to meet the diverse needs of all students more effectively. That's why having the right people on the team, each of whom has a clearly defined, established role and responsibility, is an important first step.

The Intervention Team

The school's intervention team includes a representative teacher from every grade level who functions as a case manager for the team. An RTI facilitator, ELL facilitator, speech pathologist, psychologist, and the principal make up the rest of the team. At the secondary level, the intervention team could be composed of the department chairs from each core subject area.

An active administrative presence on the team, along with staff from the special-education department, a school psychologist, and a principal, is critical to achieve appropriate interventions as early as possible.

The School Psychologist

Having the school psychologist on the team helps tremendously if a student is not making adequate progress through the RTI process and a special-education referral looks like a possibility. A psychologist who has been involved from the beginning will be familiar with the student's information and data, will have watched the student's responses to the interventions, and will have had the opportunity to provide suggestions or additional assessments to support that process. This will make the referral process to special education much smoother.

The Administration

The principal's or assistant principal's involvement on the team is critical to the whole process' success. As leaders in the school, principals guide teachers on what is important and what gets done. Richard Dufour states, "What gets monitored gets done" (Dufour and Eaker 1998). This is especially true for a school-wide process like RTI.

Having the principal or other school administrator at all the meetings shows support for the process and reinforces its level of priority. He or she provides another pair of eyes during Tier 1 instruction and provides a link when monitoring Tier 2 or Tier 3 interventions. Another benefit is that administrators can observe students during Tier 1 instruction and other non-instructional times. All of this information can be shared with the team during the meetings and used to adjust intervention plans.

The RTI Facilitator

Before we created the RTI facilitator position through a grant in our third year, our literacy specialist and principal monitored the RTI process at our school. That situation was less than ideal.

Ensuring the fidelity of all the interventions, updating the progress-monitoring tables and graphs, and keeping all the paperwork up-to-date is an overwhelming task. Even with one person designated to the job full time, it can be daunting. Without someone dedicated to these tasks, it is too easy for some students to slip through the cracks.

The RTI facilitator handles all intervention paperwork and monitoring and serves as a liaison to the teachers.

Aside from those tasks, it is beneficial if the RTI facilitator has expertise in literacy and numeracy interventions.

Our RTI facilitator supervises seven paraprofessionals and trains them on the proper delivery of skill-specific interventions. She observes the interventions and provides the paraprofessionals with feedback about the integrity of the instruction. This oversight ensures the fidelity of the process and that everything is completed.

In our school district, some schools have changed the role of their literacy specialist to that of an RTI facilitator. Depending on the budget and personnel you have available, it is beneficial to have one person at the school who oversees the entire RTI process and ensures the fidelity of the interventions and assessments.

Case Managers

Most of the intervention team consists of a representative teacher from each grade level, called a case manager. Each case manager attends all intervention team meetings and is responsible for taking the information back to his or her individual grade level to continue the conversation and make recommendations to the intervention team. This link ensures that information is disseminated to each classroom teacher and that the process continues throughout the three tiers.

Additional case manager responsibilities are as follows:

- Provide support and encouragement to the classroom teacher to assure him or her that there is a team working with him or her to help with the struggling student.
- Brainstorm and discuss at grade-level meetings ways to help students.
- Verify that the parents have been consulted and are aware of the student's academic difficulties.

- Provide the teacher with the required documentation, such as the student intervention team checklist, parent notification letter, confidential family history form (Figure 6), or the school records review form (Figure 7). (See the Appendix for all forms.)
- Ensure form completion and collection and provide them to the intervention team.
- Discuss the student's strengths and weaknesses with the teacher.
- Schedule a meeting with the RTI facilitator (or the chair of the intervention team if you do not have an RTI facilitator) to complete the RTI plan and determine interventions.
- Go over a completed student intervention plan with the classroom teacher and all involved staff.
- Follow up on progress regularly with the teacher and the intervention team.

Intervention Team Meetings

The intervention team should meet weekly or biweekly to review the graphs and make recommendations for future steps. If the progress-monitoring assessments are given weekly, the data tends to accumulate and can be overwhelming if not reviewed regularly.

Our intervention team meets every Tuesday before school starts for approximately thirty to forty minutes. Some other options:

- After-school meetings
- Common preparation time for the group once a week during the school day
- Paid, outside-of-contract time to meet

Regardless of when the team meets, meeting as frequently as possible to review the assessments and determine if the interventions are helping the students to succeed needs to be a priority.

The agenda, schedule, and format for the meetings should be established before meetings start to ensure efficiency. It is very easy to spend a lot of time discussing a student's personal history and lack of progress in the classroom if you do not adhere to a set agenda. If you focus on the data and limit the side conversations, you should be able to review the progress of many students in one meeting. (See a sample Intervention Team Agenda in the Appendix on page 97.)

Our standing agenda includes a follow-up on new students who have moved into the school along with their diagnostic assessment results. We review new students who were referred or exited in the last week, have a report from the psychologist or special-education personnel at the meeting, and spend most of the time reviewing the graphs of the Tier 2 and Tier 3 students.

We regularly rotate the grade levels to review each week. For example, the first week of the month, we start with the fifth-grade students and each week move down to the next grade level until all students have been reviewed.

During December and January, the first round of goals for the year expires, and the team makes recommendations for continuing with each student. The recommendations can vary significantly, depending on the grade level and/or student progress.

We strive for all members to agree during the decision-making process. In most cases, we are successful. However, if 100 percent consensus is not reached, we go with the majority, or the administration makes the final decision.

If members of the team cannot attend the intervention team meeting, they will send a substitute from that grade level, or they will be provided with a copy of the agenda, and another team member will catch them up on issues discussed at that meeting.

Summary

Successful RTI implementation assumes, and begins with, a functional, school-wide culture of collaboration and problem solving. The intervention team and the RTI process grow from that culture. Make sure you have the right people on the team, and they understand their roles and responsibilities. Establish a meeting schedule and an agenda, and you are ready to begin the RTI process. The first Action Step, as described in the next chapter, is to identify students who require Tier 2 or Tier 3 interventions.

IDENTIFY
STUDENTS REQUIRING TIER 2 AND TIER 3 INTERVENTION

With the intervention team in place, the first Action Step to implement RTI within a tiered intervention model is to identify which students are succeeding in Tier 1 and which are not. As noted before, identifying the struggling Tier 1 students early is extremely important. Those who are identified at the first sign of trouble and receive research-based interventions have increased chances to achieve at grade-level expectations.

It is important to note that this step in the RTI process takes place entirely in Tier 1 with all teachers and grade levels in the school, and it occurs prior to the intervention team's involvement.

Possible Tier 1 Assessment Tools

State Proficiency Exams

Teachers and administrators who work in a public school district have access to an overwhelming amount of data that can be used to identify struggling students. Since the No Child Left Behind Act of 2001 (NCLB) was passed, every public school district is required to give a yearly, state-level proficiency exam. This data alone will provide important information about your students. Whether it is a Criterion- or Norm-Referenced Test, there is a cut point or score that has already been identified as "proficient." All students under the proficiency rate could be placed on a Watch List for further identification and possible interventions.

This information, however, provides only one picture of your students' achievements on a limited amount of standards. Here are some other choices:

District-wide Assessments

Many school districts give common interim or benchmark assessments, which measure how students are learning on a set amount of standards, throughout the year. Some schools or districts even give common content exams at the end of the various instructional periods. These assessments are the next possible set of data that could be used to identify students. Team analysis of student achievement on these assessments can identify students who are not making adequate progress.

Common School Assessments

According to Rick Stiggins et.al., assessment *for* learning is one of the best ways to improve learning and to determine if students are achieving proficiency on grade-level standards. Teacher-created common assessments give an abundance of information about how students are learning. Tier 1 must include regular common assessment implementations *and* frequent teacher and administrator analyses of the assessment data to make instructional decisions. If you established a professional learning community in which departments or grade levels work together to develop common assessments, the results will provide you with a lot of information about how students are achieving (Dufour and Eaker, 1998).

Universal Screening Tools

An abundance of research supports the use of a universal screening tool, or Curriculum-Based Measurement (CBM) assessment, to identify students who are at risk for learning difficulties. The following are just a few of the hundreds of research articles that can be referred to for using a CBM that identifies students for literacy and mathematics interventions: Deno, S. L., (1985), Fuchs, L. S., Fuchs, D., Hamlett, C. L., Phillips, N. B., and Bentz, J. (1994), Shinn, M. R. and Bamonto, S. (1998), and Gersten, Clark, and Jordon, (2007).

Several CBMs are available in literacy and mathematics. The most commonly used are for early literacy skills, oral reading fluency, and computation. Several different CBM tools are available for free or for a nominal fee. Intervention Central at www.interventioncentral.org is a website to research many available CBM options and other RTI resources. The tools that are available at this site, as well as many others, provide educators with assessments that can be administered quickly and efficiently to all students in a school. Whatever CBM/universal screening tool you choose, we recommend administering it at least three times throughout the school year to provide growth measures and norm-referenced comparisons to other students throughout the nation. (See Appendix, page 12, for a list of sources for universal screening tools.)

Using Multiple Assessment Data

As noted, it's important to use multiple data sources to identify struggling students. If you limit yourself to one tool, you risk misidentification based on individual testing factors such as a bad testing day or quiet/shy students.

For example, one of our fifth-grade students continually scored low on our fluency CBM, but he was a high-achieving student who scored "Exceeded Standards" on our state proficiency test. Although he read slowly, he had outstanding comprehension of the text when he finished reading. Had we not considered multiple pieces of data, we would have run the risk of incorrectly identifying his needs.

Cut Score or Threshold

When using multiple sources of data, you need to create a "cut score" or threshold for each assessment that will be used to identify students. The score established by the state department for your state proficiency exam is a good place to start. From there, you can establish a percentage cut score for your common or district assessment (e.g., "All students who score below 60 percent on the common assessment.").

If you use classroom grades, any student earning below a C average may be considered. Universal screening tools already have levels identified for instructional recommendations. These levels are based on nationally set norms and are a good area to start for identifying at-risk students.

> Our experience reveals the wisdom gained by using a combination of data sources to increase accuracy of identification. At our school, we administer the AIMSweb Benchmarks for Early Literacy, Fluency, Early Numeracy, and Computation three times a year (www.aimsweb.com). In addition, we administer three to four common interim assessments in reading, language arts, and mathematics. All third- through fifth-grade students who score below 60 percent and all kindergarten through second-grade students who score below 70 percent on our common assessments are identified. This gives us at least seven sets of data throughout the year to monitor the progress of all K-5 students toward grade-level standards. We also use the data from our state proficiency tests in reading, writing, and mathematics for students in grades three through five. If a student falls below the proficiency threshold, we compare his or her results with the other assessments for placement on an identification list. Once students begin to receive interventions, weekly progress-monitoring assessments help us track how our students respond to the interventions.

We believe that it is not possible to have too much data on how our students learn. However, obtaining the data is not sufficient enough to make a difference. Teachers and administrators need to analyze the data regularly and make instructional decisions accordingly.

Analyzing the Data

Professional learning communities provide a forum for establishing proficiency expectations, identifying underachieving students, and analyzing student data. In fact, the results of all of the common assessments should be analyzed collaboratively as part of subject, department, or grade-level teams. Plan to set aside at least three times a year for these groups to align their expectations for mastery of content standards and to analyze closely how each student is performing in relation to those expectations.

> Tier 1 assessment is only as effective as a school's ability and willingness to use the assessment results to determine how students are achieving and thus make adjustments to their instruction.

This can be accomplished through substitute coverage, after school with extra-duty compensation, during district-scheduled staff development days, on early-release days, or other creative means of covering classes. Regardless of how this time is scheduled, it is an important step in making sure students do not slip through the cracks and thus miss extra assistance through Tier 2 or Tier 3 interventions.

Structured Teacher Planning Time

The results of the assessments we use are analyzed by each grade level as soon as the data has been disaggregated and is available. This is when you schedule the meetings between the teachers and the administration to align expectations. We call these meetings Structured Teacher Planning Time (STPT).

Our common assessments are scanned and uploaded into an instructional data management system. The data is disaggregated by state content standard as a school, a grade level, a teacher, and an individual student. During the STPT meetings, we follow a prescribed agenda beginning with the grade level's overall content standard strengths.

Identifying the strengths first allows the group to refer back to them when analyzing the weaknesses. We ask the following questions about the strengths:

1. Why do you think the students did so well on this standard?
2. What instructional strategies did you use to teach this standard?
3. How long did you spend on this area or standard?

The answers to these questions may be helpful later when the grade level looks at how to address the weaknesses. We then analyze the weaknesses of the group and compare those to its strengths. We ask some of the same questions regarding the weaknesses. We then can compare the differences and make plans for reteaching and/or interventions. This allows us to analyze each standard's instruction before we look at the individual student and his or her results.

The most valuable information is the data we have on each student indicating his or her performance in relation to each content standard. The teachers use this data to plan future instruction, review, and/or list students for possible intervention groups. As stated earlier, each student who scores below 60 percent on the common assessments is identified and placed on a list for possible Tier 2 or Tier 3 interventions. Hosting these meetings throughout the year significantly reduces the chance of missing a student who is struggling. In addition, by maintaining a list of all struggling students, you will compile a comprehensive list of all identified students by the end of the year.

The "Watch List"

We take all the data collected at the STPT meetings, analyze it in-depth, and create a list of students who may benefit from extra interventions. We call this our "Watch List." The data we use at the end of the year is a combination of our state-level proficiency exam, district end-of-year assessments, and the AIMSweb universal screening results. (See Figures 4 and 5 for sample class Watch Lists.) This information is available to all teachers at the beginning of the next school year.

> Throughout the year, at each STPT meeting, we add to the list students who fall short of the cut score, and we remove from the list students who score above the cut score at least two times throughout the year. We create a Microsoft Excel spreadsheet from the results of the common assessments of every student in the school. This spreadsheet allows us to monitor progress throughout the year and makes it easy to look for trends in a student's achievement.

Other Considerations

Every school is different when it comes to determining its students' appropriate achievement levels. Before you create your Watch Lists, factor in demographics, location, transiency, poverty levels, language acquisition, and any other student special needs. Regardless of the data or the threshold, the most important part of this step is the collaborative discussion among colleagues regarding the data and the students. Many times during these discussions, we have encountered outlier scores that we felt did not realistically reflect a particular student's achievement level. When this occurs, we put a flag on the student to remind us we need to revisit this student's data after the next common assessment.

At times, assessment data can miss a student who is struggling. When that happens, you can rely on other ways to identify students who need Tier 2 or Tier 3 interventions. For example, a student could be missing the thresholds on the common assessments by a small margin but is not being successful in the classroom. When this happens, a teacher, or even a parent, can request that the student be placed on the Watch List.

> If more than 30 percent of your students needs interventions, it is imperative to focus more of your efforts on improving Tier 1 instruction.

It goes without saying that all schools are not created equal. If your school has an unusually large number of students who are struggling, you will need to set your "cut scores" lower than a school with very few struggling students. If a school's number of students who require interventions is too high, it will not meet the needs of any of the students.

Once you complete the identification process, your next step is to diagnose the skills-deficiency problem accurately. The next chapter will provide you with ideas for diagnosing the deficiencies to help you determine where to begin the interventions.

Action Step 1

Identify students struggling with Tier 1 instruction: Decide on a combination of data sources you will use to identify struggling students, determine cut scores for each data source, and create a "Watch List" for struggling students. Our recommendation is to use a combination of data sources to increase accuracy of identification.

After this point, the intervention team will become involved and will oversee the rest of the steps in the RTI process.

Figures 4 and 5 show two different Watch Lists that we create throughout the year using our district end-of-year survey assessment, state proficiency exam, and CBM results for English/language arts and mathematics.

Name	District Survey Writing Rubric (target 70%)	District Survey Reading (target 70%)	Fluency CBM (target 61)	Nonsense Word Fluency (target 62)
Jackelyn	25	78	18	35
Irving	70	66	37	51
Victor	60	81	10	39
Asia	60	66	15	33
Nickalos	85	88	17	42
Mya	50	69	17	29
Guillermo	60	66	21	55
Nicole	65	63	10	46
Patty	80	75	16	34
Joshua	25	69	1	20
Jason	65	66	16	44
Ana	75	88	19	54
Caleb			18	23
José	70	63	22	47
David	65	75	35	50
Isaiah	30	88	19	62
Christopher	65	75	18	29
Andrew	50	59	11	31
Bryan	25	47	6	6

Figure 4: Second-grade Watch List Developed from First-grade District End-of-year Survey, and the AIMSweb CBM for Fluency and Nonsense Word Fluency for English/Language Arts

Name	State CRT (target 300)	District Survey (target 60%)	AIMSweb CBM–Computation (target 31)	AIMSweb Concepts & Application (target n/a)
Emily	297	53	33	14
Steven	243	53	18	10
Erick	297	80	20	10
Anthony	265	65	29	12
Desiree	265	68	13	6
Dennis	271	43	25	6
Kory	345	83	23	8
Nadia	309	73	33	11
Marian	297	68	30	9
Amya	276	75	31	11
Meagan	286	75	30	18
Michael	271	43	20	10
Brady	315	73	18	11
Ryan	297		27	5
Tyrell	328	68	19	10
Rosemary	303	85	37	17
Elijah	255	58	22	5
Raeleigh	336	73	15	11

Figure 5: Sample Fourth-grade Watch List Developed from the Third-grade State Proficiency Exam, District End-of-year Survey, and the AIMSweb CBM for Math Computation & Math Concepts and Applications

DIAGNOSE SKILL
DEFICIENCIES ACCURATELY

— CHAPTER FOUR —

Students struggle or fall below grade-level standards for many reasons. Figuring out exactly *why*, for many schools, is the most difficult part of the RTI process. The assessment data gathered from Chapter Three gives you some information about the specific skills students are struggling with. If that information is all that you have, you can still move forward with an intervention. However, you could still be missing some important information about a student's prerequisite skill deficit that may be the cause of his or her learning difficulties.

The Consortium on Reading Excellence, Inc. recommends, "To meet students' various assessment requirements, schools should organize their assessment toolkits around four broad types of assessments: screenings, progress monitoring, diagnostic (specific skills) assessment, and outcome assessment. In all cases, teachers need to understand the expected mastery targets for each individual skill in order to identify students who are at risk of difficulties and to tailor instructions to meet the identified needs." (CORE, 2008)

Just as a doctor will do more than check your temperature before prescribing medication, we recommend that you take a few additional measurements designed to diagnose the problems before creating an intervention plan. Don't be afraid to try several to ensure that you are choosing the right one for your students.

> Regardless of the diagnostic tool you choose, it is important to determine exactly where the skill gaps are. Providing interventions that do not address the exact skill deficit yields few positive results.

CHAPTER FOUR: Diagnose Skill Deficiencies Accurately   **19**

Diagnostic Tools

Having a good understanding of literacy and numeracy acquisition is a good place to start with diagnosis, but it is not an absolute requirement. Most reading and mathematics textbooks or basals include a form of diagnostic tool. Some resources are easier to use than others, and they offer differing depths of information. Choosing the right diagnostic tool to pinpoint skill deficiencies is an important decision. (See the Appendix for a list of websites and print references.)

> The RTI facilitator and/or paraprofessionals who work in our intervention lab administer the diagnostic assessments at our school. We use the *Assessing Reading: Multiple Measures for Kindergarten through Eighth Grade* from the CORE Literacy Training Series for diagnosing and pinpointing our literacy interventions (CORE, 2008). It offers a progressive assessment format that can be administered individually, yet is quick, reliable, and easy to use. Each assessment provides clear and accurate individual student information based on research and validation studies.
>
> For math, we rely on the AIMSweb probes. There is very little research and few resources available for mathematics diagnostics. Since we work in an elementary school, our interventions for math focus primarily on early numeracy concepts and computation. Students who leave for middle school with proficiency in addition, subtraction, multiplication, division, and a basic understanding of problem-solving traditionally have been successful in higher levels of math.
>
> When a new student enrolls in the school, previous assessment data is often not available. A school could wait to see if the student has academic difficulties or give an assessment shortly after the student begins attending school. We get excellent results by administering our diagnostic assessment to every student who transfers into the school within a few days of his or her arrival. By giving the diagnostic assessment early, we can identify concerns and begin any needed interventions immediately. The results of the diagnostic also give the classroom teacher a place to begin Tier 1 differentiated instruction.

Other Important Diagnostic Factors to Consider

Most educators often jump to the conclusion that a student is struggling because the child has a learning disability. The truth is that there are many other factors to consider when determining why there are skill deficits.

For example, while you are completing the academic diagnostic assessment, you should also complete a review of a student's educational background. Parents should complete a home health survey as well. After all, there are many factors that could be making it difficult for the student to succeed. Some additional factors to consider include:

- Poor attendance
- Transiency
- Poor instruction
- Language acquisition
- Hearing/vision impairments
- Other health risks

All these can be found by reviewing a student's cumulative records, past report cards, and home survey results. (See Figure 6 on page 22, Figure 7 on page 23, or the Appendix on pages 95 and 96 for sample forms.)

> We recommend inviting the parents/guardians to participate in a conference with the teacher to discuss past educational history and to complete the survey together. During the conference, the parent should be made aware of the process that the school is implementing and the outcome of the diagnostic assessment. Parents should be given the opportunity to give their inputs and offer their support.
>
> If it is not possible to meet with parents and complete the survey, a phone conference could be held or the form could be sent home with the child. Parent support and involvement in a child's education is a well-documented way to help a student's achievement.
>
> We recommend continuing to make an effort to have the face-to-face meeting and to keep communication lines open throughout the school year.

RESPONSE TO INTERVENTION   Confidential Family History

Date: _____ Student: _____

ID Number: _____ BD: _____ Age: _____

School: _____ Teacher: _____ Grade: _____

Parents: _____ Phone Numbers: _____

Student Health History

Concerns	Yes	No	Description of Concern
Infant			
Current			
Hearing			
Vision			
Dental			
Crawling			
Walking			
Speaking			

Check all that apply

My child

___ attended pre-school

___ attended Kindergarten

___ was retained

___ has learning problems

___ has trouble completing homework

___ has language problems

___ likes school

___ makes friends easily

___ gets mad easily

___ gets frustrated often

___ has frequent mood changes

___ is sad or cries often

___ is cooperative

Other: _____

_____

_____

Our Family

___ has experienced separation or divorce

___ has experienced family illness

___ has experienced death

___ There were medical problems during pregnancy

___ There were complications during birth

Figure 6: Confidential Family History Form

RESPONSE TO INTERVENTION

School Records Review

Date: _____ Student: _____ ID Number: _____ BD: _____ Age: _____

School: _____ Teacher: _____ Grade: _____

Student Educational History

Concerns	Yes	No	Description of Concern

Attendance Problem			Days absent/present
			    Current year _____/_____
			    Prior year _____/_____

Behavioral Problems			
Health Issues			
ELL			
Remedial Programs			
Retained			
Special Education			
Transiency			Name all schools

Parental Notification

Date	Phone	Conference	Progress Reports	Unsatisfactory Notices	Report Card

Other: _____

_____

_____

_____

_____

Figure 7: School Records Review Form

Action Step 2

Completing diagnostic probes will help determine why a student is failing to meet standards. Diagnosing specific skill deficits is one of the more difficult steps, but arguably the most important of the intervention process. Until you can identify where a student is missing the critical skills for success, your interventions will metaphorically be a shot in the dark. Begin with the students on your Watch List, administer one of many readily available diagnostic assessments, and complete school records review and confidential family history forms. In the next step, the intervention team will use the information to decide what tiered instructional level responds to the deficiencies.

CHAPTER FIVE

DETERMINING INTERVENTION LEVEL AND SETTING GOALS

With the results of the diagnosis in hand, it's time to determine the intervention levels and develop intervention plans for each student—the second most difficult step in the process.

As you analyze the results from the diagnosis, you will complete the following components of Step 3:

- Establish a goal.
- Set an Acceptable Response Threshold.
- Prioritize the skill needs.
- Determine what interventions are appropriate.
- Complete the RTI Plan for each student in Tier 3.

> By this point, it should become even more apparent that the steps are connected. The steps flow together so smoothly as they are applied that it is difficult to separate them completely.

Analyzing the Diagnosis

You can begin to determine which intervention level is appropriate for the student based on the results of the parent survey, the student's records, and the diagnostic assessment. Sometimes the assessment will determine that the student is at grade-level expectations and simply needs to continue with high-quality, Tier 1 differentiated instruction.

There are many factors to consider when determining in which tier the intervention will take place. A good rule to follow is to determine if the skill is taught within the particular grade level's Tier 1 curriculum. For example, phonemic awareness is a skill that is taught in Tier 1 at the kindergarten and first-grade levels. If a student is in second grade or higher and has a skill deficiency in phoneme segmentation, that intervention would be best addressed during a Tier 3 intervention with explicit instruction on the specific skill.

On the other hand, comprehension is a skill that is taught during Tier 1 instruction, beginning in first grade and continuing through all grades. If the student is only one grade level below on his or her comprehension level, the intervention could take place in either Tier 1 or Tier 2, depending on the severity of the discrepancy. At times, we have provided the intervention in all three tiers. A fifth-grade student could receive Tier 3 comprehension interventions at the third-grade level, Tier 2 comprehension interventions at the fourth-grade level, and Tier 1 comprehension intervention at the fifth-grade level. Therefore, if the student is only missing one or two prerequisite skills that may be at or just below his or her grade level, he or she should be placed in a Tier 2 intervention group. If the student is missing several skills and is at least one grade level below in the identified skills, he or she should be identified for Tier 3 intensive interventions.

Figures 8 and 9 show some of the typical interventions that could be completed at each grade level based on the diagnosed skill deficiency.

Interventions	Kindergarten	First Grade	Second Grade	Third Grade	Fourth Grade	Fifth Grade
Rhyming	Tier 1	Tier 2	Tier 3	Tier 3	Tier 3	Tier 3
Initial Sounds	Tier 1	Tier 2	Tier 3	Tier 3	Tier 3	Tier 3
Letter Id	Tier 1	Tier 2–3	Tier 3	Tier 3	Tier 3	Tier 3
Letter Sound	Tier 1	Tier 2–3	Tier 3	Tier 3	Tier 3	Tier 3
Segmentation	Tier 1	Tier 2–3	Tier 3	Tier 3	Tier 3	Tier 3
Deletion	Tier 1	Tier 2–3	Tier 3	Tier 3	Tier 3	Tier 3
Phonics	Tier 1	Tier 1	Tier 2–3	Tier 3	Tier 3	Tier 3
*Vocabulary	Tier 1	Tier 1	Tier 1	Tier 1–2	Tier 1–2	Tier 1–2
Fluency		Tier 1	Tier 1	Tier 2	Tier 3	Tier 3
Comprehension		Tier 1	Tier 1–2	Tier 2–3	Tier 3	Tier 3

Figure 8: Typical Interventions by Grade Level for Elementary Literacy

Interventions	Kindergarten	First Grade	Second Grade	Third Grade	Fourth Grade	Fifth Grade
Counting	Tier 1	Tier 2–3	Tier 3	Tier 3	Tier 3	Tier 3
Number Identification	Tier 1	Tier 2–3	Tier 3	Tier 3	Tier 3	Tier 3
Writing numbers	Tier 1	Tier 2–3	Tier 3	Tier 3	Tier 3	Tier 3
Addition / Subtraction	Tier 1	Tier 1	Tier 1–2	Tier 2–3	Tier 3	Tier 3
Place value		Tier 1	Tier 1–2	Tier 2–3	Tier 3	Tier 3
Multiplication / Division				Tier 1	Tier 2	Tier 3
Value of coins		Tier 1	Tier 2	Tier 3	Tier 3	Tier 3
Telling time		Tier 1	Tier 1–2	Tier 2–3	Tier 3	Tier 3

Figure 9: Typical Interventions by Grade Level for Elementary Mathematics

Creating the Tiered Instruction List

At this point, prioritize each student's skill needs and develop a plan for intervention that responds to correcting the deficiencies. A spreadsheet—done by class or grade level—indicates the results of the diagnostic assessments with each student's assigned instructional level. The list serves the following purposes:

- Records all the students that have received the diagnostic assessment at each grade level
- Helps keep track of the number of students receiving interventions at each level
- Provides a list of the interventions needed, preventing any misunderstanding of what interventions are to be provided
- Communicates to staff who work with the students the interventions and who provides them (For a sample form, see the Tiered Instruction List in the Appendix on page 98.)

Name	Tier 1	Tier 2 (Small Group)	Tier 3 (2:1 or 1:1)
Hannah	Yes	Letter Sounds, Vowels	Segmentation, Phonics 4–5D
Ricardo	Yes	No	No
Emily	Yes	Sight Words, Comprehension–third	No
Steven	Yes	Comprehension–second, Math Facts	Comprehension–second
Pricila	Yes	No	No
Suzi	Yes	Rhyming, Sight Words	Deletion, Segmentation
Anthony	Yes	Comprehension–third	No
Patricia	Yes	No	No
Desiree	Yes	Phonics 4–5F, Sight Words, Comprehension–second, math facts	Deletion, Segmentation
Christian	Yes	Comprehension–third	No
Adrian	Yes	Comprehension–second	Phonics 4–5F, SW
Roxanna	Yes	Comprehension–third	Comprehension–second
Anthony	Yes	No	No
Destiny	Yes	No	Deletion, Segmentation
Brady	Yes	Comprehension–third	Comprehension–third
Adriana	Yes	Comprehension–third	No

(continued)

Name	Tier 1	Tier 2 (Small Group)	Tier 3 (2:1 or 1:1)
Ryan	Yes	Phonics 4–5F, Comprehension–third	Comprehension–third
Eva	Yes	Sight Words, Comprehension–third	No
Elijah	Yes	Comprehension–third, Math Facts	Comprehension–second
Noah	Yes	Sight Words, Phonics 4–5F, Comprehension–third	Comprehension–third
Andrew	Yes	Phonics 4–5D	Deletion, Segmentation
Walter	Yes	No	No
Laura	Yes	Comprehension–third	Comprehension–second
Preston	Yes	Comprehension–third	Comprehension–third

Figure 10: Third-grade Tiered Instruction List from the Diagnostic Assessments

Setting Goals

Goals state the expected results for the intervention and the conditions under which the student will perform the behavior. The expected behavior should be included in the goal(s) as well as the criterion for success.

A goal should be ambitious in terms of increasing student progress, yet reasonable and practical from an instructional standpoint. Many times, it is difficult to say exactly what is ambitious and achievable; however, goals should be written based on what the average student at that particular grade level can reasonably be expected to accomplish relative to his or her peers. This can also be based on norms that have been set either nationally or for your particular area.

The criteria for success include a specific and measurable goal and an Acceptable Response Threshold (ART). An ART criterion is set to indicate the least amount of progress a student can make and still be on track for narrowing the achievement gap.

For example, a goal may be to:

Improve reading skills by mastering decoding skills in long and short vowels, blends, and digraphs by practicing one on one daily with an interventionist using flash cards and word wheels for a period of eight to twelve weeks.

Or

Improve reading and build comprehension by practicing inferencing; instruction will be daily, for a period of eight to twelve weeks, with an interventionist in a small group of three students using passages that lend themselves to making inferences.

Ideally, only one to three goals should be written at a time to address the student's areas of concern or need. The length of time a goal can be established may vary. A minimum of eight to twelve weeks is recommended, but the goal may state a considerably longer period of time. If a student is making adequate progress toward the goal, the intervention may continue to the end of the school year and/or throughout multiple years.

Along the way, the person who is implementing the intervention should monitor the progress, weekly for Tier 3 and bi-weekly for Tier 2. Reviews for adjustments to the interventions or the goals should be made approximately every three to six weeks. As a student achieves one goal, another goal may be set to continue moving the student toward grade-level standards.

Prioritize and Determine Interventions

We have already established that collaborating with colleagues, or an intervention team, is the best way to determine the goals and interventions needed. When meeting with the team, or with the referring teacher, several questions should be answered and addressed before determining the goals or writing the plan. Here are the questions that need to be addressed before determining the goals and writing each plan (See Figure 11, "Response to Intervention Plan Summary," on page 30 and the template in the Appendix on page 99):

Note that the following questions are answered for a first-grade student with beginning literacy needs.

- What is the educational concern? (Reading)
- What are the targeted skills? (Letter Identification and Letter Sounds)
- What is the baseline information for each skill? (12 percent, 0 percent)
- What type of measurement will be used? (Count correct items and convert to percentages)
- What interventions will be utilized? (Flash cards to master identification and sounds)
- What instructional method will be used? (One-on-one practice with an interventionist)
- What resources will be utilized? (Flash cards and computer assistance program)
- What interventionist will be assigned to this student? (Paraprofessional)

RESPONSE TO INTERVENTION
TIER 3
Plan Summary

Date: _____ Student: _____ ID Number: _____ BD: _____ Age: _____

School: _____ Teacher: _____ Grade: _____

Educational Concerns:	Type of Measurement:
Targeted Skills: 1. 2. 3.	

Baseline		
Skill 1	Skill 2	Skill 3

Goals (Specific statement of expected results of the intervention and the condition under which the student will perform the behavior)

1.

2.

3.

Target Goal and ART	Goal	ART
Skill 1		
Skill 2		
Skill 3		

Resources:			
Person Responsible:			

Start Date:		End Date:	
Number of Instructional Sessions	Skill 1	Skill 2	Skill 3
Minutes per Session			

Figure 11: Response to Intervention Plan Summary for Tier 3 (Also, see Appendix, page 99.)

- What goal and Acceptable Response Threshold (ART) levels will be established? (Goal is 100 percent, ART is 90 percent)
- What will be the intervention start and completion dates? (Sept. 18–Nov. 20)
- How many instructional sessions will there be for these interventions? (Fifty-three)
- What amount of time should be spent on the intervention daily? (Five to ten minutes each)

Once these questions are answered, the intervention team can begin to write the plan.

Writing the Response to Intervention Plan Summary

At this point, it is important to highlight that we only complete a formal Response to Intervention Plan Summary for students at the Tier 3 level. The planning process for students who need Tier 2 interventions is the same as Tier 3 up to this stage. However, after the goal and ART are identified, the intervention is determined, and the progress-monitoring charts are created, the formal process ends for students who need Tier 2 interventions. If the student is not successful in Tier 2 and is moved into Tier 3, the formal plan will be created. At this phase, however, the formal plan that is completed below is written for every student who is identified as Tier 3.

After prioritizing the need into goals and determining the interventions, the intervention team or case manager for that grade level will complete a written plan for every student who is in Tier 3. The written plan should be shared with all teachers and/or paraprofessionals who work with the student. In addition, parents should be informed about the plan, either in a conference or by sending a copy home. Speaking with the parent during a conference would be more beneficial, as you can identify ways that the parent can assist with the plan at home.

Action Step 3

After completing the diagnostic assessment and analyzing the outcomes, the team will create a tiered instruction list to keep accurate records of all the students assessed and their intervention levels. The next step will be to determine ambitious but achievable goals, establish an ART for a defined time period, prioritize skills needed, and determine appropriate Tier 2 and Tier 3 interventions. In addition, the team completes a formal Response to Intervention Plan Summary for each Tier 3 level intervention. (See Figure 11.)

DETERMINE AND ADMINISTER APPROPRIATE INTERVENTIONS

CHAPTER SIX

Many schools experience difficulty with this next step.

Of course, teachers know when their students are struggling, and many even know why. Schools, however, often do not believe they have the resources, time, or personnel to provide extra instruction outside of Tier 1.

We will address many of these obstacles during this chapter. We have found that Tier 2 and Tier 3 interventions are possible almost anywhere; a school is only limited by its creativity, flexibility, and determination to provide the best instruction for all students based on their individual needs.

What Is an Intervention?

Interventions should be data-driven, research-based, measurable, and based on the results of the diagnostic assessment

Some confusion exists in understanding the differences between an intervention, a modification, and an accommodation. According to the Parent Educational Advocacy Training Center (PEATC), *accommodations* are changes in *how* a student accesses information and demonstrates learning. Accommodations do not change the content or instructional level. *Modifications* are changes in *what* a student is expected to learn. Modifications may change the instructional level, the content, and/or the performance criteria.

> Remember that, by definition, an intervention is different from Tier 1 instruction and is given *in addition* to it.

Intervention has many different definitions, beginning with its primary characterization as simply "the act of intervening." In relation to the definitions of modifications and accommodations above, an intervention is a change in the *instructional strategies* delivered to accomplish the task that may, or may not, change the instructional level. An intervention is instruction that supplements and intensifies the Tier 1 classroom instruction.

You know it's an intervention when …

✓ It improves the student's skills or performance.

✓ It leads to outcomes that can be measured.

✓ It provides additional time and support to a learner.

*You know it's **not** an intervention when …*

✓ It doesn't improve student performance.

✓ It merely accommodates a student's environment or weakness.

✓ It only modifies the content of the instruction.

✓ It is only about data collection.

Accommodation	Modification	Intervention
• Priority seating • Restating directions	• Shorter passages • Adjusted grade level of passages	• Small group instruction in addition to the previous accommodation, modification, and Tier 1 instruction

Figure 12: Example of Modification, Accommodation, and Intervention for a Third-grade Student Needing Comprehension Support

RTI Intervention Considerations

With that explanation in mind, here are few intervention features to consider before you start:

- When delivering an intervention within a tiered instructional model in a school, you will want to make sure it is efficient, effective, and easy to administer.

- Most interventions can be given and practiced in fifteen minutes or fewer each day. The recommendation for the amount of time and size of the groups depends on the need of the student and the skill that he or she is practicing. It may also depend on the time, personnel, and resources that are available.

- The best way to help a student bridge the achievement gap is to begin intervening at the first area in which the student was below grade-level expectations. It is necessary to go back to this beginning skill area to fill in the gap to make sure it does not hinder his or her progress later.

- Make sure the intervention is given with integrity and fidelity at least three times a week. The RTI facilitator or building administrator will want to monitor the implementation of the interventions regularly to ensure their completion. If the student is not making gains, the first question to answer should always be, "Was the intervention implemented with fidelity and according to the plan?"

Standard Treatment or Problem-Solving Protocol?

When determining what interventions to give to students, researchers and practitioners have identified two main protocols: a Standard Treatment Protocol and a Problem-Solving Model. The Standard Treatment Protocol is designed for groups of students with similar needs, while the Problem-Solving Model is designed for individual student need.

A Standard Treatment Protocol uses pre-established intervention programs that deliver the same instruction to all students who receive it. The Problem-Solving Model creates highly individualized instruction for each student. Both systems have pros and cons.

Spending more time on skills that a student has already mastered and less on the specific, identified skill deficiencies is the shortcoming of the Standard Treatment Protocol. On the other hand, this protocol requires less training and resources to implement.

The Problem-Solving Model allows you to exactly pinpoint and address specific, identified skill deficiencies. To implement it effectively, however, you will need a good understanding of literacy and numeracy, along with extensive training on research-based strategies for teaching each individual skill. However, when using the Problem-Solving Model you can pinpoint exactly which area the student needs interventions in, and apply them in a more efficient manner.

Using a combination of both systems is the best answer. Many available intervention programs or computer software programs are good at covering and providing practice for many skills at a time. Keep in mind, however, students require specific, ongoing feedback on their progress to be successful. If you are using a computerized intervention program, the feedback may be lacking or not specific enough to ensure correction of errors in student practice.

We combine both the Standard Treatment Protocol and Problem-Solving Models. Our Tier 3 students practice their skills on a computerized intervention program (Standard Treatment Protocol) during a scheduled intervention block, during which we pull each student individually to give him or her a skill-specific intervention (Problem-Solving Model). Students get extra practice with several skills as they work on the computer, combined with a one-on-one explicit instruction format on identified weaknesses that includes specific feedback for improvement. Our Tier 2 students may work on the computer program during one part of the day and receive small-group instruction on individual skills at another time, depending on each student's diagnostic assessment.

What Interventions Are Appropriate or Research Based?

As you decide which system to use, what intervention program to purchase, or which strategies to adopt, another question arises: How do you know what program is appropriate and research-based?

Without a researcher or doctoral student on campus, it's tough for schools to keep up to date on the best and latest intervention program information. Fortunately, several sources can help. Two of our favorite sources are the What Works Clearing House and Intervention Central websites. (See the Appendix for these websites and several other program sources.)

As we read and research RTI and visit other schools to learn more about RTI implementation, we find that many educators believe that only a formal intervention program can meet the RTI requirements. However, our experience shows that may not be totally true.

The strategy of direct, explicit instruction is very often overlooked as an alternative. The Institute of Education Sciences (IES) provides two practice guides with recommendations for elementary and middle schools to implement mathematics and reading interventions (Gersten, R. et. al. 2008, 2009). These documents, which compile intervention research, recommend explicit and systematic instruction for reading and math interventions. The panel said "an intervention curriculum that covers five to six skills per day may not provide the intensity necessary to improve reading achievement." The guides can be downloaded for free from the IES and What Works Clearinghouse websites.

Most teachers know how to apply direct, explicit instruction on specific skills. We recommend utilizing the expertise available in your building. An intervention program to assist your teachers with the interventions will help with the overall practice of skills if you have the funds to purchase it. However, IES and the researchers who are referenced in their documents, recommend focusing on one to three skills with direct, explicit instruction to make the most achievement gains.

Intervention Challenges and Suggestions

Once your team has decided how to conduct the interventions, you can focus on resolving the management issues of RTI implementation. Some of the major challenges schools face are:

- Finding time within an already filled schedule
- Determining who will give the intervention
- Deciding who is going to monitor the interventions
- Supplying the Tier 1 instruction that struggling students miss when they are pulled out for interventions

These are recurrent and complex obstacles, but many schools have found creative ways to fit Tier 2 and Tier 3 interventions into their daily routines. We have provided some ideas below to help overcome some of these challenges.

Create the position of RTI facilitator. The licensed, full-time RTI facilitator position at our school was the single most beneficial factor to ensuring that the whole RTI process was implemented with fidelity. This position ensures that the students from the Watch List are diagnosed, that the plans are created, the interventions are completed, the progress-monitoring assessments are done and entered in the graphs, and that the team members are aware of their responsibilities. Before we created this position, there was not a sole person other than the principal to hold it all together. Needless to say, that failed terribly.

Schedule a daily intervention/enrichment block for each grade level. This helps overcome a few of the obstacles. With this block in place, students do not miss any new Tier 1 instruction during their intervention time. Scheduled intervention/enrichment time also allows extra personnel, such as special-education teachers, specialists, or paraprofessionals in the building, to assist with the interventions. This works best if the intervention time is staggered throughout the day for each grade level. An added benefit: our gifted students were able to receive their enriched lessons without missing regular instruction.

Hire more paraprofessionals at each grade level. Opinions about the effectiveness of paraprofessionals delivering skill-specific RTI instruction vary. We found at least one research study to support the use of paraprofessionals in the delivery of early literacy interventions (Vadasy, Sanders, and Tudor, 2007). Our paraprofessionals have successfully delivered interventions when they have been given specific training on them.

Of course, this decision is best left to each school. We have seen licensed teachers who had difficulty delivering effective interventions, and incredible paraprofessionals who implement effective interventions year after year.

Implement inclusive practices for students with disabilities. This procedure allows special-education personnel to help with all struggling students while delivering services to those students with an IEP.

> Regardless of how you overcome the obstacles, it is important to ensure that students receive their interventions at least three to five times a week, and to begin implementing them as soon as possible after the students have been identified and diagnosed.

Manipulate instructional hours. Open an intervention lab before and after school for students on campus at that time, or block schedule or stack similar classes together for increased time on a specific subject.

Trade out courses. Trading out student elective courses for intervention or remediation classes.

There are many other creative ideas that schools have implemented to fit all three instructional tiers into their schedules. As we stated earlier, a school is only limited by its flexibility and determination to make it work. Look to the resources your school has available, visit other schools that are trying different things, and commit to making it work.

Action Step 4

During this step of the RTI process, you will determine what system of intervention delivery to use: the Standard Treatment Protocol or a Problem-Solving Model. A combination of a Standard Treatment Protocol and Problem-Solving Model for interventions works well to allow for skills practice and respond to individual needs. We provided some ideas for how you can overcome RTI management challenges without a lot of money, time, or additional staff resources.

CHAPTER SEVEN

PROGRESS MONITORING

Soon after your struggling students begin their interventions, you will want to know if those interventions are working. To determine whether an intervention is effective, the team must determine the following:

- What assessments will be given
- How the assessment will be given
- Who will administer the assessment
- How often the assessment is given

> An easy-to-use format for reading and reviewing the data regularly is a must. Data gathered without a system to analyze it is useless.

Choosing the Assessment

There are many assessment choices for monitoring progress, ranging from formal to informal. Some schools prefer to use the Curriculum-Based Measurement (CBM) that was used to screen and identify students from Tier 1. These assessments are reliable and easy to administer. They are available in both literacy and mathematics skill measurements, and they are research-based. (Information on these measures is available at Intervention Central, www.interventioncentral.org.)

Many Standard Treatment Protocol interventions or software programs build periodic assessments into weekly lessons to monitor student progress. Most reading and mathematics textbook series provide intervention kits and assessment probes that are aligned with the curriculum and skills being taught.

Less formal Curriculum-Based Assessments (CBA) choices include teacher-created probes constructed directly from the instructional materials that a student is using. These assessments could also work for progress monitoring.

Whatever monitoring assessment is chosen, it should meet some important criteria. Each goal and intervention should be specific to the student or the skill he or she is working on, and the assessment used for progress monitoring should also be specifically aligned with each goal.

Some additional criteria:

- The tests match the instruction.
- The assessments are grade appropriate and quick and easy to administer.
- The assessment matches the skill level of the intervention.

To produce reliable and accurate data, the selected progress-monitoring assessment can, and should, be used for the duration of the goal.

How Are the Assessments Given, and Who Does It?

Most schools are challenged to find time to both monitor progress and find personnel to do it. Every school that encounters these challenges has its own unique way of dealing with them. The solution your school comes up with to implement the interventions will, in large part, determine how you will administer the assessments as well.

For example, if you are using an intervention block of time, you can also use that time for the assessments. The classroom teacher who administers the intervention should also assess it. If your solution was to include content specialists, interventionists, special-education personnel, or paraprofessionals in the intervention, it makes sense that they assess progress as well.

Any person in a school can assist with interventions and/or assessments. The important piece is to schedule the assessment, determine who will administer it from the beginning, and make sure there is consistent implementation.

> We include all this information in the Response to Intervention Plan Summary for our Tier 3 students. (See this template on page 99 in the Appendix.) We make sure that the person administering the intervention also administers the progress-monitoring assessment. Done this way, feedback to improve performance can be delivered more immediately, and the instruction can be adjusted as needed.

All of our Tier 3, and most of our Tier 2, interventions are completed during a 40-minute intervention block scheduled Monday through Thursday. The Tier 2 assessments are completed during that block of time on a rotating schedule for each student by the same person who administers the intervention. Each Friday, the interventionists pull their Tier 3 students from the classroom to administer their assessments one on one. This is done quickly with minimal disruption or loss of instructional time.

Every Tier 3 student subsequently has a schedule of four days of focused intervention and one day of assessment with the possibility to receive immediate feedback on progress. If we have a four-day week, the intervention is given throughout three days, with the assessment on the fourth day. Tier 2 students have a schedule with seven or nine days of intervention and one day with an assessment.

Regardless of how you schedule the assessments, you should continue to ensure the interventions take place three to five days a week.

Deciding How Often

Tier 1

Progress monitoring for Tier 1 instruction occurs on an ongoing basis through team collaboration and analysis of school-wide student assessments. As noted before, all students should be assessed three to five times a year using a universal screening tool and common assessments of the core subjects. Assessing fewer times increases the risk that struggling students will not receive the additional support they need at the Tier 2 or Tier 3 level.

Time should be set aside at least three times a year for subject departments or grade-level groups to align their expectations for content standard mastery and analysis of each student's performance in relation to those expectations. These important meetings, described in Chapter Three as "Structured Teacher Planning Time" sessions, make sure struggling students don't slip through the cracks.

Tier 2 and Tier 3

Progress monitoring in Tier 2 or Tier 3 should take place significantly more often than in Tier 1. As noted before, there is a wide range of recommendations among publications and researchers regarding implementation of Tier 2 and Tier 3 interventions. There are differences on the recommendations of the frequency of the progress monitoring as well. Some researchers recommend monitoring Tier 2 once monthly, while others recommend multiple times per week for Tier 3 progress monitoring. We recommend progress monitoring in Tier 2 every two weeks, and weekly for Tier 3. (See Figure 3, page 2.) The data collected is essential when reviewing student progress and making instructional placement decisions regarding the Response to the Intervention.

Of course, each school that implements an intervention system like this will have to choose the frequency that fits best for its resources. Once the frequency is determined for Tier 2 and Tier 3, determine the exact dates of the assessments so they can be entered onto the intervention plan prior to beginning the intervention.

> During the first three years we implemented RTI, we did not progress-monitor the Tier 2 interventions. Over time, we found that without monitoring Tier 2 interventions, we did not have documentation of their implementation, nor did we have an accurate picture of how each student transferred his or her skills to Tier 1 instruction. Monitoring the progress of the Tier 2 interventions every two weeks ensures the implementation of the intervention and gives us grouping information and more opportunities to adjust tier levels.

Organizing the Data

Keeping the data from the progress-monitoring assessments organized and readily available for review can be challenging. The format should be easy to use, allow for accurate analysis, and be accessible to all staff working with the students.

Most CBM tools have a separate progress-monitoring option within their program that will create a graph from the data. You may find, however, that the universal screening tools offer limited assessment choices. For more flexibility in assessing more specific skills, you will need to find another option.

A spreadsheet program, such as Microsoft Excel, offers an easy way to generate tables and graphs to input student scores. The graphs are automatically generated.

During Step 4, "Determine and Administer Appropriate Interventions," the intervention goal and the ART were established, as well as an accurate baseline from the diagnostic assessment.

With those in place, the last thing you will need to do to acquire the information for the table is determine all the progress-monitoring test dates. (Figure 13 shows a sample table that was created for tracking letter identification. Figure 14 shows the graph that was generated from the table for letter identification.)

	G	ART	Goal
Dates	**100**	**90**	**Letter Identification**
Base			12
Test Dates			
Sept 18	100	90	27
Sept 25	100	90	58
Oct 2	100	90	58
Oct 9	100	90	67
Oct 16	100	90	81
Oct 23	100	90	86
Nov 6	100	90	89
Nov 13	100	90	100
Nov 20	100	90	100

Figure 13: Sample Excel Table for Progress-Monitoring Letter Identification

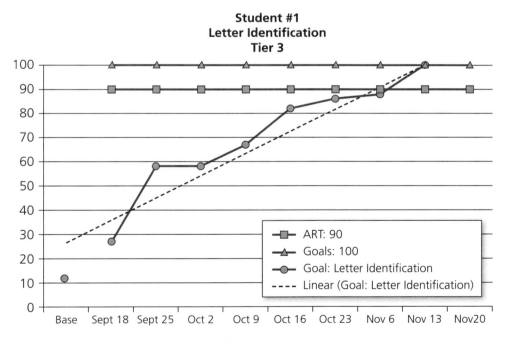

Figure 14: Progress-Monitoring Graph for Letter Identification

We maintain all the tables for the Tier 2 and Tier 3 progress-monitoring assessments in a file on a shared network drive at our school. By making the files accessible to all staff members, the data from the assessments can be entered at any time from any computer in the school, and individual student progress can be reviewed at any time. The files are saved and backed up each day to ensure the security of the data. Our intervention team reviews the graphs electronically, which saves a lot of paper. At the end of the intervention period, we print a copy of each student's graphs and file them in a three-ring binder.

Action Step 5

During this step, a school intervention team will determine what assessment to use, who will administer it, how he or she will administer it, how often it will be given, and how the data will be managed. The assessments need to be reliable, easy to administer, and aligned with the intervention. We recommended organizing the data into a format that is easily accessed and graphed. All of these guidelines will help you determine if the interventions are working.

ANALYZE
THE DATA

— CHAPTER EIGHT —

If you have been following the steps in this book, you now have charts and graphs with an abundance of data about your students' performances from their Tier 2 and Tier 3 interventions.

All this data will be useless if you don't have a team and a plan to analyze the assessment information on a regular basis. When we set the goals in Chapter Five, we indicated that the length of the intervention should continue for a minimum of eight to twelve weeks, but that some could go on much longer. We also recommended that you review the progress of the intervention about every three to six weeks. This chapter takes you through the process of analyzing the data to make the important decisions regarding the next steps.

Reviewing the Data

As the intervention team reviews the progress of students' responses to the interventions, note that there are a few different perspectives to consider that lend to the outcomes. The following are the different questions that team members answer from their individual perspectives:

The Classroom Teacher
- Was the problem diagnosed appropriately?
- Was the goal appropriate?
- Did the intervention address the concern?
- Was the intervention fully implemented?
- How much progress did the student make?
- Can the problem be resolved within the classroom setting?
- What action is recommended for continuing?

The Intervention Team and Administration
- Were the Tier 2 and Tier 3 interventions provided with integrity and fidelity?
- Did we provide support to the teachers and students during Tier 2 and Tier 3 interventions?

- Did we provide ongoing staff development for research-based interventions?
- Did we assess the interventions frequently enough for adequate progress monitoring?
- Did we review the progress of each student frequently enough to determine if the interventions were working?

The Psychologist Perspective

- Did the student respond to the interventions at an appropriate rate and at an adequate level compared to his or her peers?
- Did the monitoring include functional instructional data; curriculum-based material, and standardized testing?
- Did this data fulfill the evaluation criteria mandated in IDEIA?
- Did we identify a framework to develop appropriate programming?
- Did we help the child?

After answering the above questions, the intervention team will make recommendations for continuing. The recommendations, of course, will depend on the answers to the questions and if the problems were resolved.

Possible Outcomes

Now that you have data to show how your students are responding to the interventions, there are decisions that you need to make regarding how to continue. Several outcomes could occur, depending on the answers to the above questions and the data. The outcomes usually fall into one of three categories: problem resolved, being resolved, or unresolved. Within each of the three outcomes are recommended actions that can take place.

Problem Resolved

If the student is making progress and has achieved his or her goals, the instructional problem is on its way to being resolved. You will want to establish a decision rubric at this point to help determine the next steps.

A good rule to follow is if a student has reached his or her goal for three consecutive data points, the student should be moved from Tier 3 to Tier 2, create new goals, and continue to monitor progress every two weeks. If the student achieves his or her goal for three consecutive data points at Tier 2, the student should be moved from Tier 2 to Tier 1.

It's a good idea to place the student on the Watch List and continue to monitor progress on common assessments until he or she achieves success at grade-level standards for approximately a year. It is very important to reduce the interventions and progress monitoring incrementally to make sure that the student is successful before he or she is removed altogether.

Being Resolved

This outcome means that the student is making progress but has not achieved his or her goal. At this point, there are two options: continue interventions and monitoring at their current levels, or create a new goal and make minor adjustments to the interventions.

For example, if the student is working on comprehension strategies at a level below his or her grade level, increase the instructional level. We do this sometimes to increase the expectation of students and push them to close the achievement gap. If you make this change, it is important to document it on the progress-monitoring graphs by making a vertical line at the date of the change and entering the change. (See Figure 15.)

If the change is successful, you can continue the process until the student meets the new goal. If the student does not make progress on the new goal, simply make the adjustment back to the previous goal, and continue with the intervention.

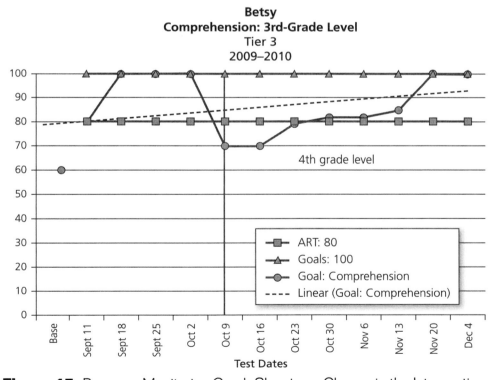

Figure 15: Progress-Monitoring Graph Showing a Change in the Intervention

Unresolved

If the student is not making gains or is not achieving at an adequate rate to close the achievement gap, the problem is unresolved. The first thing to consider is his or her placement in the intervention tiers. If the student is in Tier 2, your first option is to move him or her to Tier 3, create new goals, change the interventions, complete the RTI Summary Plan, and continue to monitor progress. Changes can be made to the frequency, duration, instructional level, intensity, or the size of the small group.

If the student is already in Tier 3 interventions and you have made changes to the intervention, your next option is to consult with your school psychologist for short-term cognitive, academic, language, or behavioral assessments.

Depending on the outcome of these assessments, the team can decide to continue as is with the interventions and progress monitoring. If the team decides that the interventions are continuing to be unsuccessful, the next options to consider are full referral for special-education services, a Section 504 plan, or retention.

This re-evaluation process continues for as long as the students need the extra support. Some students can make gains in filling small skill gaps and then return exclusively to Tier 1 instruction within a short time frame. Others make progress in Tier 3, move to Tier 2, and then to Tier 1 within a single school year. A few students will even move back and forth throughout the tiers for several years.

The possibilities are only restricted by the resources available, the time put into them, and the desire to have all students succeed.

Action Step 6

The intervention team will frequently need to make some important decisions based on the data. If students are achieving or making progress toward their goals, they should be moved into the next level of interventions. All students should be able to move fluidly between the tiers based on the data and their individual needs.

The Action Steps end here, but, of course, the process continues and should become part of your school's culture. At our school, RTI is simply a matter of "how we do business" to make sure that all our students can succeed.

APPLYING
THE ACTION STEPS

The process of integrating RTI as part of your school's culture actually begins with the creation of a school-wide collaboration and team problem-solving. After that, the RTI Action Steps are the following:

- **Step 1:** Identify Students Struggling With Tier 1 Instruction.
- **Step 2:** Diagnose Skill Deficiencies Accurately.
- **Step 3:** Set Goals and Create a Plan for Interventions.
- **Step 4:** Determine and Administer Appropriate Interventions.
- **Step 5:** Monitor Progress.
- **Step 6:** Analyze Data and Determine Possible Outcomes.

Remember that the steps overlap and, for some students, may continue for many years. Students should be able to move fluidly between and through the tiers, depending on the outcomes of either the progress-monitoring or common school-wide assessments.

The individual case studies that follow illustrate how the steps work. Each takes you through all six steps and shows how the identification process and outcome for each student will differ.

The first case study follows the progress of José, a first-grade student who arrived at our school from Mexico with very limited English speaking or reading skills. After one year of intervention, he caught up with his peers and was ready to continue in Tier 1.

The second case study details the interventions for Freddy, another English-language learner (ELL). Unlike José, Freddy did not receive appropriate interventions at the school he previously attended. Once he came to our school as a fourth-grader and we administered a diagnostic assessment to determine his needs, he made approximately two years of growth in his first year of interventions.

The third case study describes a three-year process of interventions that began in the first grade for Jess that, in the fourth year, resulted in referral for special-education eligibility.

Case Study 1: José

José enrolled as a first-grader at our school at the beginning of the year. He had moved to our area from Mexico, where he had attended kindergarten. His native language was Spanish, and he came to us speaking very little English.

Action Step 1: Identify Students Struggling with Tier 1 Instruction

Because José was new to the United States and our school, he was automatically identified for the Watch List and moved to Step 2 of diagnosis. In Chapter Four, we described how we give the diagnostic assessment to all new students who enroll so that we immediately know if a student will need any interventions.

Action Step 2: Diagnose Skill Deficiencies Accurately

The RTI facilitator gave José the Assessment Sequence for Primary Grade Students from the *CORE Assessing Reading, Multiple Measures for Kindergarten through Eighth Grade.* The following were his results:

Phonological Awareness Screening Test
Rhyming–0 percent
Initial Sounds–20 percent
Segmentation–0 percent
Deletion–0 percent

CORE Phonics Survey
Letter names–13 percent
Letter sounds–0 percent

Phonics-Reading and Decoding skills
Vowels, CVC, Blends, Digraphs, Long Vowels Patterns, R-Controlled Vowels, Variant Vowels and diphthongs–0 percent

Fry Oral Reading Test (Fluency)
Beginning first-grade level–1A

Critchlow Verbal Language Scales (Vocabulary)
Below kindergarten level

Assessment of Reading Comprehension
(Not assessed due to grade level)

Results of the Diagnostic Test

José was a perfect example of the English-language learner (ELL) who regularly enrolls in many schools throughout the United States. His lack of English vocabulary presents a challenge that needs to be addressed immediately.

As with all ELL transfers, we began building José's English vocabulary by teaching the deficit skills at the first area where they were below grade-level expectations. For José, those areas were in phonological awareness and phonics-alphabet skills.

Although the diagnostic test indicated limited knowledge in other areas of reading, these were not addressed because those skills are taught during Tier 1 instruction in first grade.

Action Step 3: Set Goals and Create a Plan for Interventions

Tier 3 Interventions

The diagnostic assessment showed José's first area of concern was in phonological awareness. Although this skill is covered during Tier 1 instruction in first grade, he scored significantly lower than his peers in segmentation. Consequently, Tier 3 interventions were given to catch José up with his peers. The Tier 3 interventions were provided one on one, during the scheduled intervention block, by a paraprofessional, four days a week, for ten to fifteen minutes a session.

The low phonics-alphabet skills are addressed as a review in the regular first-grade classroom during Tier 1 instruction. Since José was significantly behind his peers in this area, he received additional Tier 3 interventions, working one on one with a paraprofessional four days a week, for about ten minutes each session, at the same time he worked on segmentation skills.

The interventions were set up for twelve weeks and were assessed weekly to track progress. The intervention team reviewed results about every three to six weeks. When he met his goal three weeks in a row, the interventions were reduced or eliminated.

Phonological awareness, in segmentation, should be mastered at 100 percent accuracy by the end of third grade. Since we maintain high expectations, the goal was set at 100 percent, but the Acceptable Response Threshold (ART) was set at 75 percent. Phonics-alphabet skills should be mastered by the beginning of first grade; consequently, the goal and the ART were both set at 100 percent.

Tier 2 Interventions

José was also below grade-level expectations in rhyming, initial sounds, and deletion, which are phonological awareness skills taught in first grade during regular Tier 1 instruction. Because José scored significantly lower than his peers in these areas, however, he received Tier 2 interventions in the regular education classroom during the scheduled reading time. The teacher, special-education inclusion teacher, or paraprofessional worked with a small group of homogeneously grouped students to develop these skills.

A formal Response to Intervention Plan Summary was not written for the Tier 2 interventions. However, progress-monitoring graphs were created to track the results. José was assessed every other week for these goals by the person who delivered the intervention. His progress was reviewed every three to six weeks by the intervention team, and the intervention was modified, intensified, or eliminated as necessary. When he reached his goal three weeks in a row, the intervention was reduced or eliminated.

Formal Response to Intervention Plan Summary for Tier 3 Interventions

At this point, a formal Response to Intervention Plan Summary was completed for the Tier 3 interventions and assessments. In addition, José's parents were sent a letter indicating that their child would be receiving interventions. Because José was a new student at the school, and had been administered the diagnostic assessment his first week, the classroom teacher scheduled a parent conference after this point to share the information. (See Figure 16 and the Appendix on page 99.)

Action Step 4: Determine and Administer Appropriate Interventions

Tier 3 Interventions

José needed direct, explicit instruction and practice in segmentation and phonics-alphabetic skills.

A paraprofessional introduced and demonstrated the skills. José had guided practice on the skills and was asked to demonstrate the skills independently.

RESPONSE TO INTERVENTION
TIER 3

Plan Summary

Date: _____ Student: _Josè_____ ID Number: _____ BD: _____ Age: _____

School: _____ Teacher: _____ Grade: _____

Educational Concerns: *Reading*	Type of Measurement: *No. correct converted to %*

Targeted Skills:

1. *Segmentation*

2. *Phonics-Letter Identification*

3. *Phonics-Letter Sounds*

Baseline

Skill 1	Skill 2	Skill 3
0%	*13%*	*0%*

Goals (Specific statement of expected results of the intervention and the condition under which the student will perform the behavior)

1. *Improve reading skills by mastering the phonological awareness skill of segmentation. He will practice one on one with an intervention specialist daily touching one finger for each sound he hears in a word.*

2. *Improve reading skills by mastering letter identification. José will practice one on one with an intervention specialist daily, using flash cards to practice identifying each letter.*

3. *Improve reading skills by mastering letter sounds. José will practice one on one with an intervention specialist daily, using flash cards to practice generating each letter sound.*

Target Goal and ART	Goal	ART
Skill 1	*100%*	*75%*
Skill 2	*100%*	*100%*
Skill 3	*100%*	*100%*

Resources: *segmentation practice sheet and alphabet flash cards*

Person Responsible: *Intervention Specialist*

Start Date: *9-21-09*		End Date: *1-6-10*	
Number of Instructional Sessions	Skill 1 *60*	Skill 2 *60*	Skill 3 *60*
Minutes per Session	*10*	*10*	*10*

Figure 16: The Response to Intervention Plan Summary for the Tier 3 Intervention

One way to practice segmentation is to have students simply use their fingers. José was asked to touch a finger for each sound he heard in a word. A variety of words were used to practice CVC words, blends, digraphs, long vowel patterns, r-controlled vowels, and variant vowels.

Some effective strategies with phonics-alphabet skill interventions are flash cards to practice identifying letters and their associated sounds.

Tier 2 Interventions

The Tier 2 deletion, rhyming, and initial sound interventions were administered by the teacher in the regular classroom in a small group of one to three students using direct, explicit instruction. She introduced the skills systematically and demonstrated their correct uses.

> The classroom teacher or the paraprofessional can administer the Tier 2 interventions.

José practiced deletion with a white board so he could easily see which letters were deleted and which remained. Picture cards and puzzles were used to practice rhyming and to practice initial sounds. The teacher named the picture and generated the beginning sound for any unknown letters, with José repeating the letter name or sound.

Documentation for Tier 2 and Tier 3 Interventions

The Tier 3 interventions were listed on the Response to Intervention Plan Summary. The Tier 2 and Tier 3 interventions were documented on the tiered instruction list that was posted on a shared network site where all school staff had access. The lists are posted to ensure that all teachers and/or paraprofessionals know their roles and responsibilities.

Action Step 5: Monitor Progress

Progress-Monitoring Assessments

As we established the interventions during Step 4, the RTI facilitator determined what progress-monitoring tests would be used to track the student's progress. The assessments selected for José were the *CORE Phoneme Segmentation Test and the CORE Phonics Survey Form*. These tests matched the instruction and were quick and easy to give and to grade.

Gathering and Inputting Information into the Excel Spreadsheet

After completing the Response to Intervention Plan Summary, we set up the charts and graphs in an Excel spreadsheet. The goal, Acceptable Response Threshold, and all the dates for the assessments were entered. The baseline data was retrieved from the diagnostic assessment and entered into the spreadsheet before beginning the interventions.

This is the way José's graphs looked at the beginning of the intervention period. At this point, the baseline is the only score. (All baseline graphs look this way at the beginning of the intervention process.)

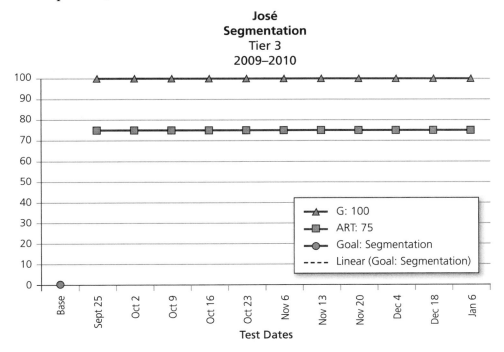

Figure 17

This is what the Tier 3 table and graph looked like after the assessment results were entered. Scores were entered every week in the table so a new data point would be displayed on the graph.

	G	ART	goal	G	ART	goal	G	ART	goal
Dates	100	75	Segmentation	100	100	Letter Identification	100	100	Letter Sounds
Base			0			13			0
Test Dates									
25-Sep	100	75	53	100	100	25	100	100	4
2-Oct	100	75	60	100	100	36	100	100	25
9-Oct	100	75	80	100	100	48	100	100	29
16-Oct	100	75	67	100	100	58	100	100	43
23-Oct	100	75	80	100	100	69	100	100	71
6-Nov	100	75	87	100	100	92	100	100	89
13-Nov	100	75	100	100	100	94	100	100	79
20-Nov	100	75	93	100	100	100	100	100	96
4-Dec	100	75	100	100	100	100	100	100	100
18-Dec	100	75	100	100	100	100	100	100	100
6-Jan	100	75	100	100	100	100	100	100	100

Figure 18: (For a blank table, see the Tracking Table form in the Appendix on page 100.)

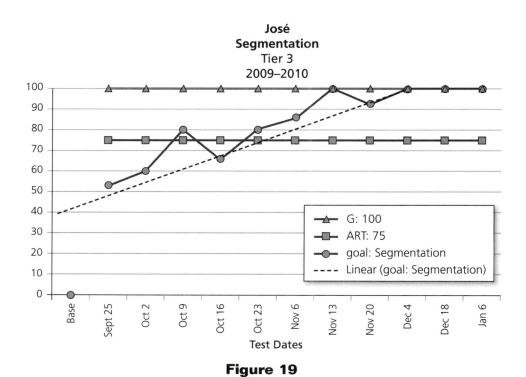

Figure 19

By the ninth, tenth, and eleventh weeks, José had achieved the 100 percent goal for segmentation.

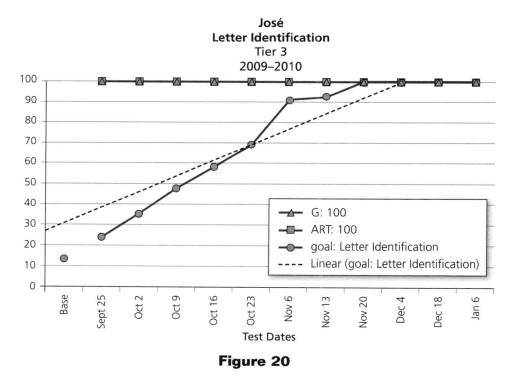

Figure 20

José had achieved his goal of 100 percent on letter identification in the eighth, ninth, tenth, and eleventh weeks.

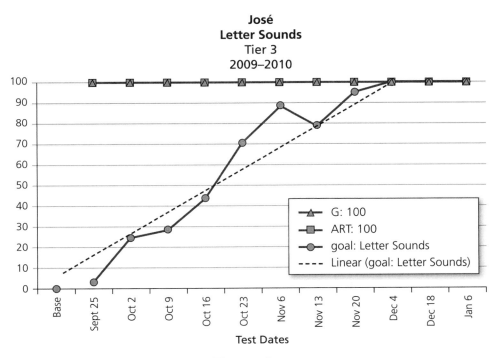

José
Letter Sounds
Tier 3
2009–2010

Legend:
- G: 100
- ART: 100
- goal: Letter Sounds
- Linear (goal: Letter Sounds)

Test Dates

Figure 21

The results from this Tier 3 intervention show that in the ninth, tenth, and eleventh weeks, José achieved his goal of 100 percent on letter sounds.

Each week, a score was entered in the Tier 2 table so a new data point would be displayed on the graph.

	G	ART	goal	G	ART	goal	G	ART	goal
Dates	**100**	**80**	**Rhyming**	**100**	**80**	**Initial Sounds**	**100**	**75**	**Deletion**
Base			0			20			0
Test Dates									
Sep 18	100	80		100	80	67	100	75	85
Oct 2	100	80	50	100	80	33	100	75	100
Oct 16	100	80	20	100	80	100	100	75	100
Nov 6	100	80	50	100	80	94	100	75	100
Nov 20	100	80	25	100	80	100	100	75	100
Dec 4	100	80	50	100	80	100	100	75	
Dec 18	100	80	17	100	80	100	100	75	
Jan 8	100	80	100	100	80		100	75	
Jan 22	100	80	100	100	80		100	75	
Feb 5	100	80	100	100	80		100	75	
Feb 26	100	80	100	100	80		100	75	
Mar 12	100	80		100	80		100	75	
Apr 16	100	80		100	80		100	75	
Apr 30	100	80		100	80		100	75	
May 14	100	80		100	80		100	75	
May 28	100	80		100	80		100	75	

Figure 22

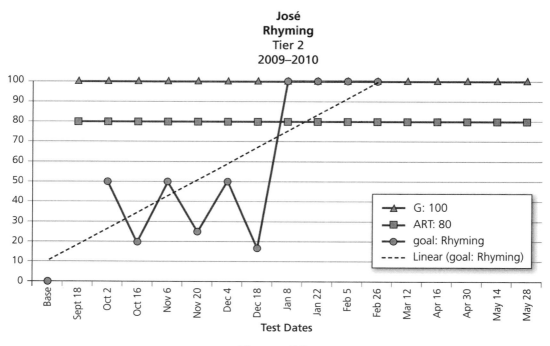

Figure 23

The results from this Tier 2 intervention show that in the seventh, eighth, ninth, and tenth weeks, José achieved his goal of 100 percent in rhyming.

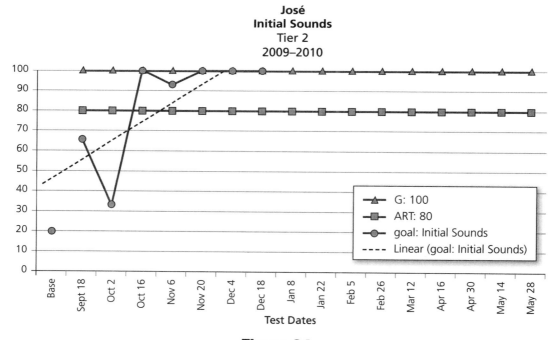

Figure 24

The results from this Tier 2 intervention show that in the fifth, sixth, and seventh weeks, José achieved his goal of 100 percent on initial sounds.

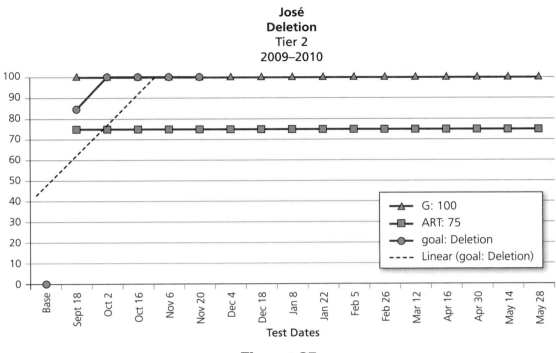

Figuret 25

The results from this Tier 2 intervention show that in the second, third, fourth, and fifth weeks, José achieved his goal of 100 percent on deletion.

Action Step 6: Analyze Data and Determine Possible Outcomes

José's Tier 2 and Tier 3 progress was reviewed every three to six weeks. At the sixth week, the intervention team noted the progress of all the Tier 3 interventions and one of the Tier 2 interventions, but continued the interventions until the goals were achieved.

At the eleventh week, the intervention team decided to discontinue the Tier 3 interventions, because José had achieved the goals.

By the seventh week of the Tier 2 intervention, José had achieved his goal of initial sounds. By the tenth week, he had achieved the rhyming goal, and by the fifth week, he had achieved the deletion goal.

José was removed from both Tier 2 and Tier 3 interventions.

At the completion of the school year, José's end-of-the-year school district survey assessment in English language arts was 63 percent. Although José scored seven percentage points below our cut point of 70 percent for first grade, he made significant gains in acquiring language and was working on first-grade skills during Tier 1 instruction. José will be on the Watch List for the next school year so we can continue to monitor his progress and intervene if necessary.

Case Study 2: Freddy

Freddy began his fourth-grade year with us on the first day of school. His primary language was Spanish, and he came to us with limited English. He had attended first through third grade at another school in our district, and he had been retained once in third grade. Freddy received an intervention during both years he attended third grade, but not before that time. His records transferred with him, and we noted several problems related to his previous interventions.

- A diagnostic assessment was not completed to determine appropriate interventions.
- The intervention (reading CVC and CCVC words with fluency) was inappropriate because he did not have the prerequisite skill (letter sounds) needed to be successful.
- The intervention was progress-monitored but was not reviewed frequently enough.
- When the progress was reviewed, and was obviously not bridging the gap, there were no adjustments made to the intervention.
- Only one intervention was ever administered.

Action Step 1: Identify Students Struggling With Tier 1 Instruction

Since Freddy was new to our school, he was automatically identified for the Watch List and moved to Step 2 diagnosis.

Action Step 2: Diagnose Skill Deficiencies Accurately

A paraprofessional gave Freddy the Assessment Sequence for Primary Grade Students from the *CORE Assessing Reading: Multiple Measures for Kindergarten through Eighth Grade*. The following were his results:

Phonological Awareness Screening Test
Segmentation–53 percent
Deletion–75 percent

CORE Phonics Survey
Letter names–83 percent
Letter sounds–61 percent

Phonics-Reading and Decoding Skills
Vowels, CVC, Blends, Digraphs, Long Vowels Patterns, R-Controlled Vowels, Variant Vowels and diphthongs–32 percent

Fry Oral Reading Test (Fluency)

Beginning first-grade level–1B

San Diego Quick Assessment of Reading Ability (Sight Words)

Pre-primer

Critchlow Verbal Language Scales (Vocabulary)

14–second-grade level

Assessment of Reading Comprehension 1

First-grade level

Results of the Diagnostic Test

As with José, Freddy was a perfect example of an English-language learner who regularly enrolled in many schools throughout the U.S. He lives in a home where his exposure to English is minimal. His lack of English vocabulary presented a challenge that needed to be addressed immediately.

As we did with José, we began building Freddy's English vocabulary and teaching the deficit skills at the first area in which he was below grade-level expectations. The results of his diagnostic assessment showed us that Freddy had deficits in phonological awareness, phonics-alphabet skills, phonics reading and decoding skills, fluency, sight words, and comprehension.

All of these deficit skills on this lengthy list were addressed, and interventions were provided during his fourth-grade year, with the exception of fluency—fluency was above the skills that he was working on and would be added when he had the prerequisite reading skills.

Action Step 3: Set Goals and Create a Plan for Interventions

Tier 3 Interventions

The diagnostic assessment showed Freddy's first area of concern was in phonological awareness in segmentation. In fourth grade, this skill is not covered during Tier 1 instruction. Consequently, Tier 3 interventions were given to ensure success and to catch him up with his peers. The Tier 3 interventions were provided one on one by a paraprofessional, four days a week, for ten to fifteen minutes per session, during the scheduled intervention block.

The second area of concern, phonics-alphabet skills, was not covered during Tier 1 instruction in fourth grade either. Consequently, he received Tier 3 interventions. Freddy worked on his phonics skills one on one with a paraprofessional, four days a week, for about ten minutes per session at the same time he was working on the segmentation skills.

Sight words, Freddy's third area of concern, were a skill covered during fourth-grade Tier 1 instruction. Freddy scored significantly lower than his peers in the sight words area, however. Consequently, he received Tier 3 interventions.

Due to the severe gaps in his skills, all of Freddy's Tier 3 interventions were set up for fifteen weeks. The interventions were assessed weekly to track his progress. Progress was reviewed every three to six weeks by the intervention team. When he met his goal three weeks in a row, the interventions were reduced or eliminated.

Phonological awareness, in segmentation, should be mastered at 100 percent accuracy by the end of third grade. Because Freddy is in the fourth grade, the goal was set at 100 percent, and the Acceptable Response Threshold (ART) was set at 90 percent. Phonics-alphabet skills should be mastered by the beginning of first grade. Again, the goal was set at 100 percent, but the ART was set at 90 percent.

By the beginning of fourth grade, Freddy should have been on sight word group twenty-five according to the Fry Sight Words lists. Since he was beginning on sight word group two (the second group of the first-grade list), his goal was set at sight word group fifteen, and the ART was set at thirteen.

Tier 2 Interventions

Freddy was also below grade-level expectations in phonics and decoding skills. As these skills are not addressed in the fourth-grade classroom at his level during regular Tier 1 instruction, Tier 2 interventions were given. Freddy worked on his phonics skills one on one with the classroom teacher or paraprofessional, four days a week, for about ten minutes per session during the regular Tier 1 reading block. Usually, in Tier 2 the student would be in a small group of homogeneously grouped students. But Freddy received one-on-one instruction because no one else was at his level.

A formal RTI Summary Plan was not written for the Tier 2 intervention; however, a progress-monitoring graph was created to track the results of the intervention. Freddy was assessed every other week for this goal. His progress was reviewed every three to six weeks, and the intervention was modified, intensified, or eliminated as necessary. When he reached his goal three weeks in a row, the intervention was reduced or eliminated.

Formal Response to Intervention Plan Summary for the Tier 3 Interventions

At this point, a formal Response to Intervention Plan Summary was completed for the Tier 3 interventions and assessments. Figure 26 on page 64 is the Response to Intervention Plan Summary for the Tier 3 interventions:

Action Step 4: Determine and Administer Appropriate Interventions

Tier 3 Interventions

In segmentation, phonics-alphabetic skills, and sight words, Freddy needed direct, explicit instruction and practice. A paraprofessional introduced each skill and demonstrated how to do it correctly. Freddy had guided practice and was asked to demonstrate the skill independently.

Freddy practiced segmentation by lining up paper clips and was asked to touch a paper clip for each sound he heard in a word. A variety of words were used to practice CVC words, blends, digraphs, long vowel patterns, r-controlled vowels and variant vowels.

Flash cards were used to practice identifying letters and their associated sounds for the phonics-alphabet skills as well as to identify sight words.

Tier 2 Interventions

The classroom teacher administered the Tier 2 phonics interventions in the regular classroom one on one using direct, explicit, and systematic instruction, introducing the skills and modeling how to do them correctly. The initial strategy for practicing phonics asked Freddy to state the vowels and voice their long and short sounds. Next, flash cards were used to introduce blends and digraphs. Finally, word wheels were used to read words with short vowels in CVC words, short vowels with blends, and digraphs and long vowels in long vowel spellings. The paraprofessional generated any unknown sounds and decoded the unknown words, and Freddy repeated the unknown sounds or words.

Documentation for Tier 2 and Tier 3 Interventions

The Tier 3 interventions were listed on the Response to Intervention Plan Summary, which eliminated confusion about the type of instruction Freddy should receive. The Tier 2 interventions were documented on the tiered instruction list that was posted on a shared network site where all school staff had access to them.

RESPONSE TO INTERVENTION		Plan Summary
	TIER 3	

Date: _____ Student: _Freddy_ ID Number: _____ BD: _____ Age: _____

School: _____ Teacher: _____ Grade: _____

Educational Concerns: *Reading*	Type of Measurement: *No. correct converted to %*		
Targeted Skills:			
1. *Segmentation*			
2. *Letter Sounds*			
3. *Sight Words*			
Baseline			
Skill 1	**Skill 2**		**Skill 3**
53%	*61%*		*Fry Sight Word Group 1*

Goals (Specific statement of expected results of the intervention and the condition under which the student will perform the behavior)

1. *Freddy will improve his reading skills by practicing segmentation 1:1 daily with a teacher, isolating each individual sound in words*

2. *Freddy will improve his reading skills by practicing letter sounds with flash cards 1:1 daily with a teacher.*

3. *Freddy will improve his reading skills by building a sight word vocabulary. He will practice 1:1 daily with a teacher reading sight words from flash cards.*

Target Goal and ART	Goal	ART
Skill 1	*100%*	*90%*
Skill 2	*100%*	*90%*
Skill 3	*Group 15*	*Group 13*

Resources: *Segmentation practice sheet, paper clips, alphabet flash cards, and Fry Sight Words flash cards*

Person Responsible: *Intervention Specialist*

Start Date: *9-24-10*		End Date: *2-8-11*	
Number of Instructional Sessions	Skill 1 *75*	Skill 2 *75*	Skill 3 *75*
Minutes per Session	*10*	*10*	*10*

Figure 26: The Response to Intervention Plan Summary for the Tier 3 Intervention

Action Step 5: Monitor Progress

Progress-Monitoring Assessments

While we were establishing the interventions during Step 4, the RTI facilitator also determined what progress-monitoring tests would be used to track Freddy's progress.

The assessments selected for Freddy were the *CORE Phoneme Segmentation Test, the CORE Phonics Survey Alphabet Skills Record Form, Fry Sight Words lists and CORE Reading and Decoding sheet.*

Gathering and Inputting Information into the Excel Spreadsheet

After completing the Response to Intervention Plan Summary, we set up the charts and graphs in an Excel spreadsheet. The goal, ART, and the dates of the assessments were entered. The baseline data was retrieved from the diagnostic assessment and entered into the spreadsheet before beginning the interventions.

This is the way that Freddy's Tier 3 graphs looked at the beginning of the intervention period. At this point, the only score is the baseline. All the baseline graphs will look this way at the beginning.

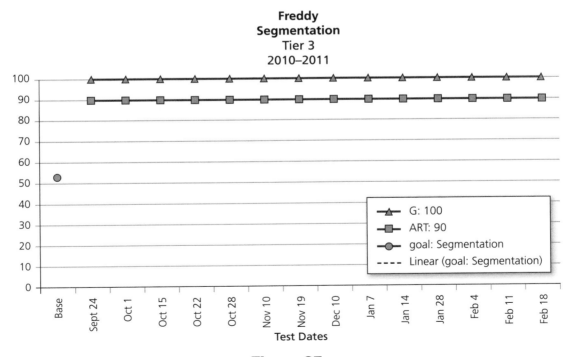

Figure 27

This is what the Tier 3 table and graphs looked like after the assessment results were entered. Each week, a score was entered in the table so a new data point would be displayed on the graphs.

Dates	G 100	ART 90	goal Segmentation	G 100	ART 90	goal Letter Sounds	G 15	ART 13	goal Sight Words
Base			53			61			1
Test Dates									
Sep 24	100	90		100	90	92	15	13	2
Oct 1	100	90	53	100	90	84	15	13	2
Oct 15	100	90	80	100	90	82	15	13	2
Oct 22	100	90	73	100	90	79	15	13	3
Oct 28	100	90	93	100	90	100	15	13	3
Nov 10	100	90	87	100	90	92	15	13	4
Nov 19	100	90	87	100	90	96	15	13	4
Dec 10	100	90	60	100	90	100	15	13	5
Jan 7	100	90	80	100	90	100	15	13	6
Jan 14	100	90	87	100	90	100	15	13	6
Jan 21	100	90	87	100	90		15	13	7
Jan 28	100	90	100	100	90		15	13	7
Feb 4	100	90	100	100	90		15	13	8
Feb 11	100	90		100	90		15	13	8
Feb 18	100	90		100	90		15	13	9

Figure 28: (For a blank table, see the Tracking Table form in the Appendix on page 100)

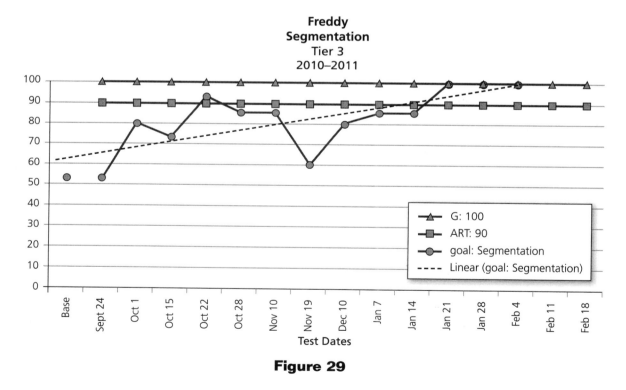

Figure 29

The results from this Tier 3 intervention show that Freddy achieved this goal in the eleventh, twelfth, and thirteenth weeks.

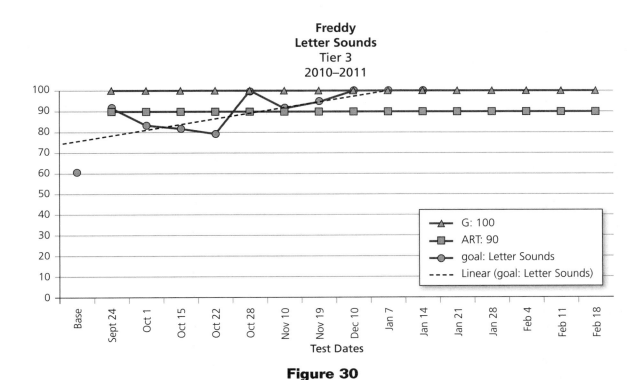

Figure 30

The results from this Tier 3 intervention show that Freddy achieved his goal in the eighth, ninth, and tenth weeks.

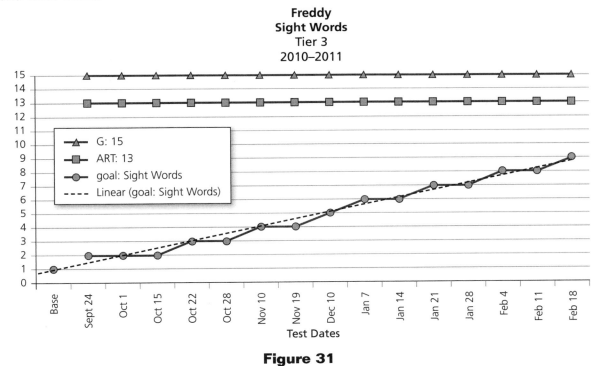

Figure 31

The results from this Tier 3 intervention show that Freddy made progress, but he did not achieve this goal.

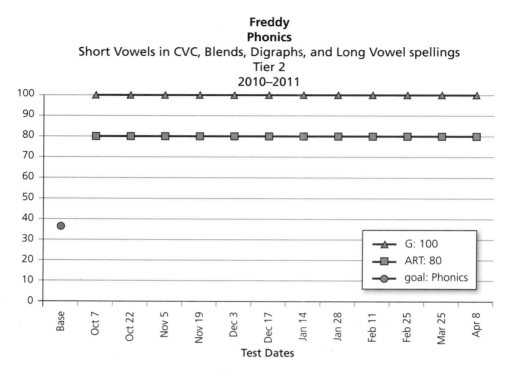

Figure 32

This is the way that Freddy's Tier 2 graph looked at the beginning of the intervention period. At this point, the only score is the baseline. All the baseline graphs will look this way at the beginning.

	G	ART	goal	G	ART	goal	G	ART	goal
Dates	100	80	**Phonics**						
Base			37						
Test Dates									
Oct 7	100	80	82						
Oct 22	100	80	58						
Nov 5	100	80	64						
Nov 19	100	80	76						
Dec 3	100	80	80						
Dec 17	100	80	84						
Jan 14	100	80	88						
Jan 28	100	80	100						
Feb 11	100	80	96						
Feb 25	100	80	60						
Mar 25	100	80	92						
Apr 8	100	80	94						

Figure 33

This is what the Tier 2 table and graph looked like after the assessment results were entered. A new score was entered on the table each week.

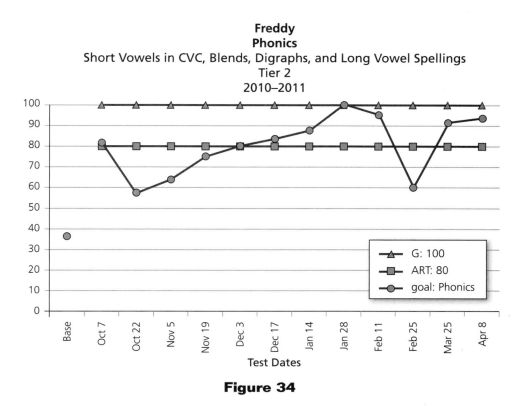

Freddy
Phonics
Short Vowels in CVC, Blends, Digraphs, and Long Vowel Spellings
Tier 2
2010–2011

Test Dates

Legend:
- G: 100
- ART: 80
- goal: Phonics

Figure 34

The results from this Tier 2 intervention show that Freddy scored between the ART and the goal in six of the last seven data points.

Action Step 6: Analyze Data and Determine Possible Outcomes

Freddy's progress was reviewed in approximately the sixth and twelfth weeks. In the sixth week, the intervention team noted the reading progress in segmentation and letter sounds but continued the intervention until Freddy reached his goal three times in a row. It noted the slow progress in sight words and decided to continue the intervention with increased intensity. The team continued the Tier 2 intervention and increased the intensity there as well.

By the tenth week, the team decided to remove Freddy from letter sounds, and by the thirteenth week, the team exited Freddy from segmentation.

It was time to establish some new goals, so based on the progress made on the first goals, the intervention team decided to continue the sight words goal in Tier 3 interventions and move the phonics goal from Tier 2 to Tier 3. The phonics goal was expanded. Additionally, a new comprehension intervention was started in Tier 2.

Because Freddy was already identified and placed on the Watch List and a diagnostic assessment was completed at the beginning of the year, we will go directly to Action Step 3 for Freddy's second goals.

Action Step 3: Set Goals and Create a Plan for Interventions

Tier 3 Interventions

Freddy's sight words continued to be an area of concern, with Freddy still scoring significantly lower than his peers. Consequently, Tier 3 interventions continued.

The interventions were set up for an additional ten weeks, with a weekly assessment to track progress. Progress was reviewed every three to six weeks by the intervention team. When Freddy met his goal three weeks in a row, the interventions were reduced or eliminated.

Freddy had made progress during the first goal period in phonics and decoding skills, but he was still lagging behind his peers. Consequently, Tier 3 interventions were given. Freddy worked on his phonics skills one on one, with a teacher or paraprofessional four days a week, for about ten minutes per session, during the scheduled intervention block.

By the beginning of fourth grade, Freddy should have been on sight word group twenty-five, according to the Fry Sight Words lists. After the first goal period, Freddy was on group nine of the Fry Sight Words. His second goal for sight words was set at group nineteen, and the ART was set at seventeen. The phonics goals were expanded to include r- and l-controlled vowels, variant vowels, and diphthongs. His goal was set at 100 percent and a 90 percent ART.

Tier 2 Interventions

Freddy was also below grade-level expectations in comprehension. Even though this skill is addressed in the fourth-grade classroom, Freddy required additional support at his reading level. Consequently, Tier 2 interventions were given to ensure success and to catch him up with his peers. Freddy worked on his comprehension skills one on one with a teacher or paraprofessional four days a week, for about ten minutes per session during the regular Tier 1 reading block. Usually in Tier 2, students would work in a small group of homogeneously grouped students. Freddy received one-on-one instruction because no one else was at his level.

A formal RTI goal sheet was not written for the Tier 2 intervention. However, a progress-monitoring graph was created to track the results of the intervention. Freddy was assessed every other week for this goal. His progress was reviewed every three to six weeks, and the intervention was modified, intensified, or eliminated as necessary. When he reached his goal three weeks in a row, the intervention was reduced or eliminated.

At this point, another formal Response to Intervention Plan Summary was completed for the Tier 3 interventions and assessments. The following is the Response to Intervention Plan Summary for the Tier 3 interventions:

RESPONSE TO INTERVENTION   **Plan Summary**

TIER 3

Date: _____ Student: _*Freddy*_ ID Number: _____ BD: _____ Age: _____

School: _____ Teacher: _____ Grade: _____

Educational Concerns: *Reading*	Type of Measurement: *No. correct converted to %*

Targeted Skills:

1. *Sight Words*

2. *Phonics*

Baseline

Skill 1	Skill 2	Skill 3
Fry Sight Word Group 9	*74%*	

Goals (Specific statement of expected results of the intervention and the condition under which the student will perform the behavior)

1. *Freddy will improve his reading skills by building a sight word vocabulary. He will practice 1:1 daily with a teacher reading sight words from flash cards.*

2. *Freddy will improve his reading skills by practicing decoding skills with short vowels in CVC words, words with blends and digraphs, long vowel spellings, r- and l-controlled vowels, variant vowels and diphthongs 1:1 with and interventionist daily using flash cards and word wheels.*

Target Goal and ART	Goal	ART
Skill 1	*Group 19*	*Group 17*
Skill 2	*100%*	*90%*
Skill 3		

Resources: *Fry Sight Words flash cards, phonics flash cards, and word wheels*

Person Responsible: *Intervention Specialist*

Start Date: *3-25-11*		End Date: *6-3-11*	
Number of Instructional Sessions	Skill 1 *50*	Skill 2 *50*	Skill 3
Minutes per Session	*10*	*10*	

Figure 35: Response to Intervention Plan Summary for the Tier 3 Intervention

Action Step 4: Determine and Administer Appropriate Interventions

Tier 3 Interventions

Freddy needed direct, explicit instruction and practice in sight words and phonics. An effective strategy to use with sight words is flash cards. The paraprofessional introduced the skills and demonstrated how to read the words correctly. Freddy had guided practice on this skill and was asked to demonstrate the skill independently.

In phonics, Freddy needed direct instruction and practice in decoding. He worked one on one with a paraprofessional. Some strategies that were used for phonics interventions were flashcards to practice the sounds in isolation, nonsense word flash cards, and word wheels. A variety of words were used to ensure adequate practice reading words with blends, digraphs, long and short vowels, r-controlled vowels, variant vowels, and diphthongs.

Tier 2 Interventions

The Tier 2 comprehension intervention was administered one on one by the classroom teacher. A new passage or story at the second-grade level was selected for use each week. During Tier 2 interventions, much attention was given to strategies to assist in building comprehension. For example, pre-reading strategies were used to develop vocabulary, build background knowledge, and bring awareness to what the passage or story was about. While reading, Freddy was asked to visualize what he was reading, he was asked probing questions to ensure ongoing comprehension. Upon completion of the passage or story, he was asked open-ended questions or to retell the story or make up a new ending. Instruction each week focused on a different strategy to ensure plenty of practice with each before moving on to a new one.

Documentation for Tier 2 and Tier 3 Interventions

The Tier 3 interventions were listed on the Response to Intervention Plan Summary. The Tier 2 intervention was documented on the tiered instruction list that was posted on a shared network site where all school staff had access to them.

Action Step 5: Monitor Progress

Progress-Monitoring Assessments

While we were establishing the interventions during Step 4, the RTI facilitator determined what progress-monitoring tests would be utilized to track Freddy's progress.

Freddy used the Fry Sight Words lists and CORE reading decoding sheet. A variety of comprehension passages at the second-grade level were also chosen.

Gathering and inputting information into the Excel spreadsheet

After completing the Response to Intervention Plan Summary, we set up the charts and graphs in an Excel spreadsheet with all the required information for completing the progress monitoring. The goal, ART, and the dates of the assessments were entered. The baseline data was retrieved from the diagnostic assessment and entered into the spreadsheet before beginning the interventions.

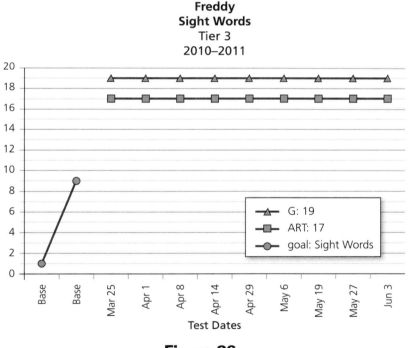

Figure 36

This is the way that Freddy's graphs looked at the beginning of the intervention period. At this point, the score shows his previous growth and the new baseline. All the baseline graphs will look this way when creating new goals.

	G	ART	goal	G	ART	goal	G	ART	Goal 3
Dates	19	17	Sight Words			Phonics			
Base			1			36			
Base			9			74			
Test Dates									
Mar 25	19	17	10	100	90	73			
Apr 1	19	17	11	100	90	78			
Apr 8	19	17	12	100	90	78			
Apr 14	19	17	12	100	90	85			
Apr 29	19	17	13	100	90	92			
May 6	19	17	13	100	90	89			
May 19	19	17	13	100	90	94			
May 27	19	17	14	100	90	100			
Jun 3	19	17	15	100	90	100			

Figure 37: (For a blank table, see the Tracking Table form in the Appendix on page 100.)

This is what the Tier 3 table and graph looked like after the assessment results were entered.

	G	ART	goal	G	ART	goal	G	ART	Goal 3
Dates	19	17	Sight Words						
Base			20						
Test Dates									
Mar 25	100	80							
Apr 8	100	80							
Apr 29	100	80							
May 13	100	80							
May 27	100	80							

Figure 38

This is what the Tier 3 table and graph looked like after the assessment results were entered.

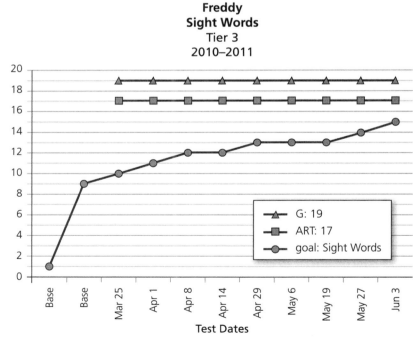

Freddy
Sight Words
Tier 3
2010–2011

The results from this Tier 3 intervention show that Freddy made progress, but he did not achieve this goal.

Figure 39

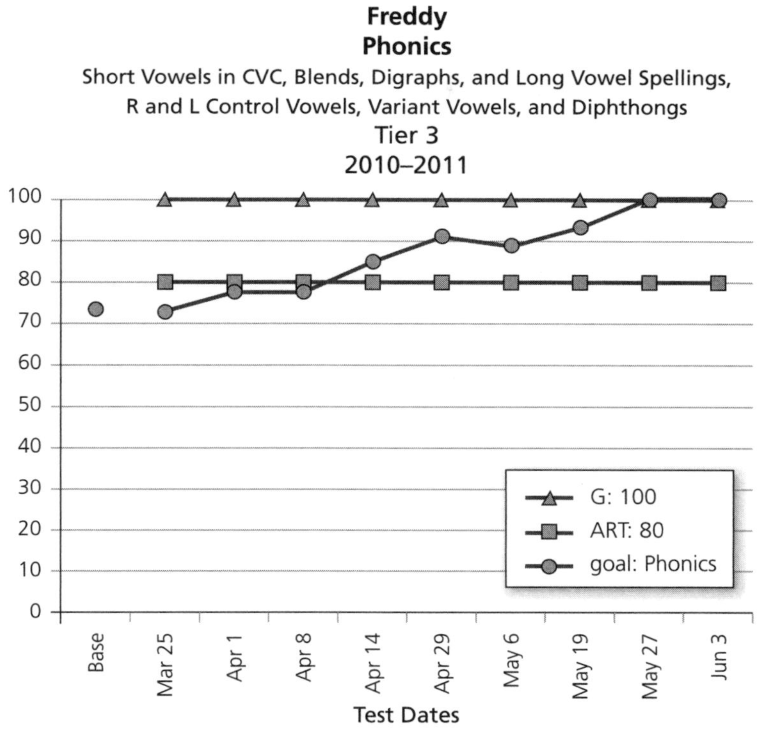

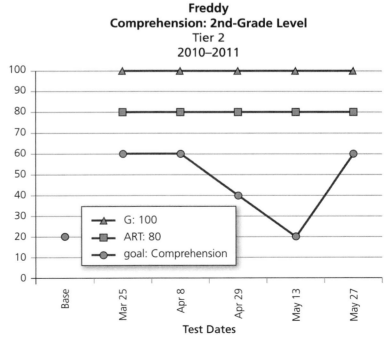

Freddy
Phonics
Short Vowels in CVC, Blends, Digraphs, and Long Vowel Spellings, R and L Control Vowels, Variant Vowels, and Diphthongs
Tier 3
2010–2011
100
90
80
70
60
50
40
30
20
10
0
G: 100
ART: 80
goal: Phonics
Base
Mar 25
Apr 1
Apr 8
Apr 14
Apr 29
May 6
May 19
May 27
Jun 3
Test Dates

Figure 40

The results from this Tier 3 intervention show that Freddy achieved his goal on the last two data points.

Freddy
Comprehension: 2nd-Grade Level
Tier 2
2010–2011
100
90
80
70
60
50
40
30
20
10
0
G: 100
ART: 80
goal: Comprehension
Base
Mar 25
Apr 8
Apr 29
May 13
May 27
Test Dates

Figure 41

The results from this Tier 2 intervention show that Freddy made some inconsistent progress, but he did not achieve this goal.

Action Step 6: Analyze Data and Determine Possible Outcomes

Freddy's progress was reviewed at the sixth and tenth weeks. At the sixth week, the intervention team noted the reading progress in sight words and phonics, but continued the intervention until Freddy reached his goal three times in a row. The team noted the slow and inconsistent progress in the Tier 2 comprehension intervention and decided to continue the intervention with increased intensity.

By the tenth week, the team noted the progress on sight words. Despite the increased intensity, Freddy did not make his goal. Freddy did achieve his goal in phonics, while he continues to struggle with comprehension.

Although Freddy did not achieve all his goals during his fourth-grade year, the intervention team and his classroom teacher were pleased with his growth. He completely achieved his goals in segmentation, letter sounds, and phonics. In sight words, he achieved his ART. His comprehension intervention fell short of success, but we hope next year his comprehension will improve because he has now mastered many of the prerequisite skills necessary to improve his reading skills.

Freddy came to us with a lot of catching up to do after being retained, plus having an inappropriate intervention for a full school year. He also struggled with language deficits. In addition to all of Freddy's other interventions, he worked on computerized language programs. Even though Freddy is still working substantially below grade-level expectations, he did make approximately two years of growth during one year of interventions. Freddy will be placed on our Watch List for the next school year. He will be placed in interventions right away to give him every opportunity to continue to bridge his achievement gap.

Case Study 3: Jess

Jess illustrates an example of how a student can move fluidly through the intervention tiers for several years. After four years of interventions, Jess ultimately was referred for special-education testing and was found eligible. The most important aspect of this study is that Jess received the interventions she needed throughout the entire four years. She did not have to wait until she was found eligible to get help. A brief review of her progress during the first three years appears below under the first Action Step. Her fourth year, during which she was referred for special education, will be described in detail in the remaining Action Steps.

Action Step 1: Identify Students Struggling With Tier 1 Instruction

Jess began first grade at our school on the first day of the school year. By the end of the first semester, however, during the STPT meeting of the first-grade teachers, there were some concerns about her progress, and she was placed on the Watch List. A CORE diagnostic assessment showed Jess at or very close to grade-level expectations in all areas. Consequently, no further action was taken during her first-grade year.

Jess did not do well on the end-of-the-year district survey, however, scoring 49 percent in English language arts. When she returned for second grade, the RTI facilitator met with her classroom teacher; goals were written and interventions were provided in phonological awareness (segmentation) and sight words. The following are her graphs from the beginning of her second-grade year:

Jess achieved her goals in both areas, but she continued to struggle with comprehension, scoring a 44 percent on her second-grade district end-of-the-year survey assessment in English language arts.

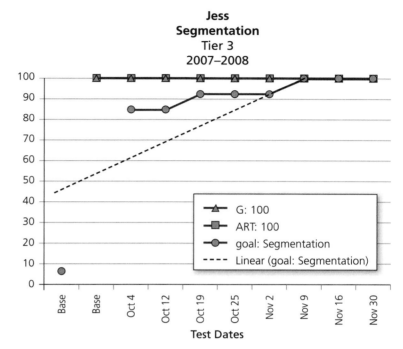

Figure 42

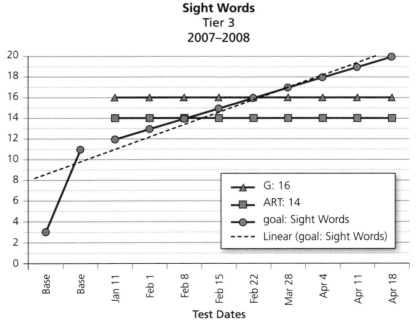

Figure 43

At the beginning of her third-grade year, Jess scored at or near grade-level expectations in all areas except comprehension and vocabulary on another CORE diagnostic assessment. Goals were written and interventions were provided for vocabulary development and comprehension. These interventions were provided with increasing intensity, but there was very little progress as the following graphs show:

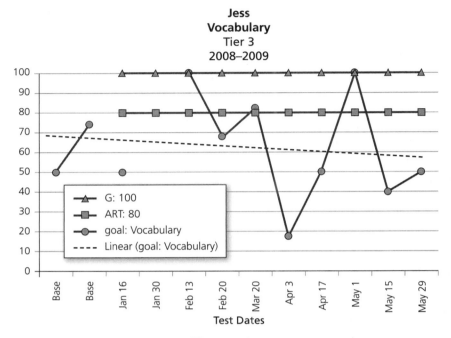

Figure 44

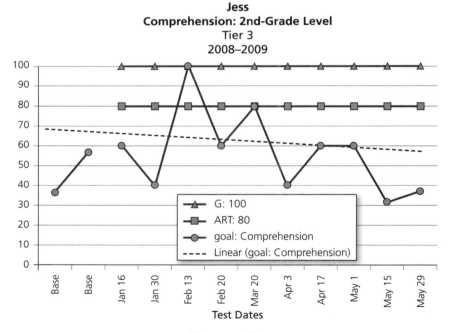

Figure 45

Once again, Jess scored 53 percent on her third-grade district end-of-the-year survey assessment in English language arts, and on the Nevada Criterion-Referenced Test (CRT) in reading she scored a 216. (A score of 300 is required to be considered proficient.) Jess scored 45 percent on her third-grade district end-of-the-year survey assessment in math, and on the Nevada Criterion-Reference Test (CRT) in math she scored a 195. As she entered fourth grade, we administered a third CORE diagnostic assessment. We knew Jess was struggling in math as well. We administered an informal math diagnosis and found three areas of concern. The results of her assessment follow.

Action Step 2: Diagnose Skill Deficiencies Accurately

At the beginning of fourth grade, Jess was given the third *Assessment Sequence for Upper Grade Students* from the CORE Literacy Training Series. The following were her results:

Phonological Awareness Screening Test:
Rhyming – 100 percent
Initial Sounds – 100 percent
Segmentation – 52 percent
Deletion – 100 percent

CORE Phonics Survey
Vowels, CVC, Blends, Digraphs, Long Vowels Patterns, R-Controlled Vowels, Variant Vowels and diphthongs–68 percent

Fry Oral Reading Test (Fluency)
Sixth grade

Critchlow Verbal Language Scales (Vocabulary)
First grade

Assessment of Reading Comprehension
Late second grade

Math Informal Diagnosis:
Math facts: Addition/Subtraction Recall
2's addition and subtraction
Reading Numbers to the Millions' Place
60 percent
Writing Numbers to the Millions' Place
100 percent

Results of the Diagnostic Test:

Although many students fall behind because of transiency and absences, this was not the case with Jess. She had been at our school for four years and during that time had received a tremendous amount of support. We were quite concerned about her lack of progress. We held several parent conferences throughout the years to discuss Jess' progress, and we were aware that Jess had been diagnosed with Attention Deficit Hyperactivity Disorder (ADHD). During her fourth-grade year, Jess began taking medication for ADHD.

The results of the current diagnostic assessment showed that Jess continued to have gaps in phonological awareness in segmentation, phonics, vocabulary, and comprehension, despite the progress in these areas she had made the previous years.

The results from our informal math diagnosis indicated that Jess also struggled with number sense in math facts, and reading and writing numbers to the millions' place. Jess had received small-group, differentiated instruction for her mathematics deficits, but we realized that we needed to intensify the interventions to close the gaps in her learning.

The RTI facilitator and her classroom teacher determined the level of interventions that would be required, and goals were written to create the intervention plan. Although we did not usually have students work on more than two or three goals at one time, we expanded the level of assistance Jess was receiving due to her poor progress.

Action Step 3: Set Goals and Create a Plan for Interventions

The diagnostic assessment showed that Jess was still below grade-level expectations in the phonological awareness skill of segmentation. The deficient skills had been taught during Tier 1 instruction in kindergarten and first grade, so we went back to that level to fill in the gaps.

Since this skill would require practice that would not be provided in the regular classroom during Tier 1 instruction, Jess received support with segmentation in Tier 3 interventions. She received one-on-one instruction from a paraprofessional four times a week, for five to ten minutes a session.

The diagnostic assessment also showed that Jess scored below grade-level expectations in phonics, lacking decoding skills taught mostly in Tier 1 instruction during the third grade. Since this skill would also require more practice than would be provided in the regular classroom during Tier 1 instruction, Jess received additional support in phonics during Tier 3 interventions.

She received one-on-one instruction by a paraprofessional four times a week, for five to ten minutes a session, during the same time she was working on the segmentation skills.

Both of these interventions were scheduled for twelve weeks, and they were assessed weekly by the same person who had delivered the intervention. The intervention team reviewed and tracked her progress and made intervention adjustments as needed. The goal was set at 100 percent.

Because the diagnostic assessment also showed that Jess was more than a year below grade-level expectations and had struggled with comprehension for more than one school year, she also received this intervention in Tier 3 interventions. This was given in addition to comprehension instruction during her Tier 1 reading time, and a Tier 2 small-group intervention.

She worked on fourth-grade comprehension skills and passages during Tier 1 instruction. The Tier 2 and Tier 3 interventions were completed using third-grade passages and assessments. A teacher or paraprofessional worked with a small group of homogeneously grouped students during Tier 2 interventions to build comprehension strategies.

The interventions were scheduled for twelve weeks, and she was assessed weekly on the Tier 3 interventions, and biweekly on the Tier 2 interventions. Her progress was reviewed every three to six weeks by the intervention team and modified as needed. A formal goal sheet was not written for the Tier 2 interventions; however, we did set up progress-monitoring graphs to track the results of the intervention.

In addition, the informal math diagnostic assessment showed that Jess was still below grade-level expectations in numbers sense, specifically in math facts and reading/writing numbers to the millions' place. The math fact skills that she was lacking were significantly below the fourth-grade level. Since these skills would require practice that would not be provided in the regular classroom during Tier 1 instruction, Jess received support with math facts and reading/writing numbers to the millions' place in Tier 3 interventions. A paraprofessional gave her one-on-one instruction four times a week, for five to ten minutes a session.

Note that Jess' baseline for writing numbers to the millions' place was 100 percent. However, from previous assessments and teacher observation, we were not convinced Jess had mastered the skill, so we opted to administer the intervention and to progress-monitor writing numbers to the millions' place until she displayed evidence of mastery.

RESPONSE TO INTERVENTION
TIER 3
Plan Summary

Date: _____ Student: _Jess_____ ID Number: _____ BD: _____ Age: _____

School: _____ Teacher: _____ Grade: _____

Educational Concerns: *Reading*	Type of Measurement: *No. correct converted to %*

Targeted Skills:
1. *Segmentation*
2. *Phonics*
3. *Comprehension*

Baseline

Skill 1	Skill 2	Skill 3
52% at a third-grade level	*68%*	*40%*

Goals (Specific statement of expected results of the intervention and the condition under which the student will perform the behavior)

1. *Improve reading skills by mastering the phonological awareness skill of segmentation. Practice one on one with an intervention specialist touching one finger for each sound he hears in a word.*

2. *Improve reading skills by mastering decoding skills-blends, digraphs, long and short vowels, r-controlled vowels, variant vowels and diphthongs. Practice one on one with an intervention specialist using phonics flash cards, nonsense words and word wheels.*

3. *Improve reading skills by practicing reading strategies to build comprehension. Practice the following comprehension strategies with an intervention specialist in a small group of 1-3 students four days a week:*
   - *Visualize what you are reading*
   - *Ask what do you picture as you are reading the passage*
   - *Connect to background information*
   - *Ask questions/make connections. Make inferences*
   - *Answer who, what, when, where, and why questions*
   - *Answer story element questions*
   - *Ask about facts*
   - *Students underline the answer in the passage*

Target Goal and ART	Goal	ART
Skill 1	*100%*	*100%*
Skill 2	*100%*	*100%*
Skill 3	*100%*	*80%*

Resources: *1) Segmentation practice sheet and paper clips; 2) Phonics flash cards, nonsense word flash cards, & word wheels; 3) Third-grade passages for practice and testing*
Person Responsible: *Intervention Specialist*

Start Date: *9-21-09*		End Date: *12-04-09*	
Number of Instructional Sessions	Skill 1 *58*	Skill 2 *58*	Skill 3 *58*
Minutes per Session	*10*	*10*	*15*

Figure 46: Response to Intervention Plan Summary for Tier 3 Intervention

At this point, a formal Response to Intervention Plan Summary was completed for the Tier 3 interventions (Figure 47 on page 84).

Action Step 4: Determine and Administer Appropriate Interventions

Tier 3 interventions

In phonological awareness and phonics, Jess needed direct instruction and practice with segmentation. Because direct, explicit, and systematic instruction is the best method for teaching this skill, the teacher or a paraprofessional introduced the skill and demonstrated how to do it correctly. Jess had guided practice on this skill and was asked to demonstrate the skill independently.

One way Jess practiced segmentation was to use her fingers. She would be asked to touch a finger for each sound she heard in a word. A variety of words, such as CVC words, blends, digraphs, long vowel patterns, r-controlled vowels, and variant vowels, were used to practice. Some strategies that were used for phonics interventions were flashcards to practice the sounds in isolation, nonsense word flash cards, and word wheels. A variety of words was used to ensure adequate practice reading words with blends, digraphs, long and short vowels, r-controlled vowels, variant vowels, and diphthongs.

The Tier 3 comprehension intervention was administered in a small group of one to three students by a paraprofessional. A new passage or story at the third-grade level was selected each week. Much attention was given to strategies to assist in building comprehension. For example, pre-reading strategies were used to develop vocabulary, build background knowledge, and bring awareness to what the passage or story was about. During reading, Jess was asked to visualize what she was reading. She was asked probing questions to ensure ongoing comprehension. Upon completion of the passage or story, she was asked open-ended questions or was asked to retell the story or to make up a new ending. Instruction focused on a different strategy each week to ensure plenty of practice before moving on to a new one.

In number sense, Jess needed direct instruction and practice in addition and subtraction of math facts. The teacher or paraprofessional introduced each fact family and reviewed all facts. Facts that Jess had difficulty with were given additional practice time. Jess was given guided practice on each fact family until she demonstrated mastery.

RESPONSE TO INTERVENTION   **Plan Summary**

TIER 3

Date: _____ Student: _Jess_____ ID Number: _____ BD: _____ Age: _____

School: _____ Teacher: _____ Grade: _____

Educational Concerns: _Reading_	Type of Measurement: _No. correct converted to %_

Targeted Skills:

1. _Math Facts_

2. _Reading Numbers to the Millions' Place_

3. _Writing numbers to the Millions' Place_

Baseline

Skill 1	Skill 2	Skill 3
2's add and 2's sub	_64%_	_100%_

Goals (Specific statement of expected results of the intervention and the condition under which the student will perform the behavior)

1. _Improve math skills by improving number sense and mastering addition and subtraction math facts. Jess will practice one on one with an intervention specialist using flash cards and practice sheets._

2. _Improve math skills by reading numbers to the millions' place. Jess will practice one on one with an intervention specialist reading numbers from flash cards._

3. _Improve math skills by writing numbers to the millions' place. Jess will practice one on one writing numbers as they are dictated to her._

Target Goal and ART	Goal	ART
Skill 1	_9 addition, 12 subtraction_	_9 addition, 12 subtraction_
Skill 2	_100%_	_80%_
Skill 3	_100%_	_100%_

Resources: _Math facts flash cards and Flash Master handheld device; 2) Practice sheets and numbers flash cards to the millions' place_

Person Responsible: _Intervention Specialist_

Start Date: _3-25-11_		End Date: _6-3-11_	
Number of Instructional Sessions	Skill 1 _68_	Skill 2 _68_	Skill 3 _68_
Minutes per Session	_10_	_10_	_10_

Figure 47: Response to Intervention Plan Summary for the Tier 3 Intervention

One way Jess practiced math facts was with flash cards and practice sheets. She also practiced them independently with a handheld *Flash Master*. Once she completed a timed practice sheet in the time designated appropriate for her with 100 percent accuracy, she was moved to the next fact family.

In number sense, Jess also needed direct instruction and needed to practice reading and writing numbers to the millions' place. The teacher or paraprofessional demonstrated how to correctly read and write each number. Jess was then asked to read and write numbers for the interventionist. Numbers she had difficulty with were given additional practice time. Jess was given practice reading and writing numbers from the hundreds' place to the millions' place. In addition, the teacher or paraprofessional carefully pointed out each number's place value. Jess was given guided practice reading and writing numbers until she demonstrated mastery.

Tier 2 Interventions

The Tier 2 comprehension intervention was administered in a small group of four to six students. A new passage or story at the third-grade level was selected each week. The strategies used were the same as the Tier 3 intervention but were provided by a different interventionist. This double-dosing of skills' instruction gave Jess multiple opportunities to apply her skills in comprehension and transfer them to the Tier 1 instruction.

The Tier 3 interventions were listed on the Response to Intervention Plan Summary. The Tier 2 interventions were listed on the tiered instruction list that was posted on a shared network site where all school staff has access to them.

While we were establishing the interventions, the RTI facilitator determined what progress-monitoring tests would be utilized to track the student's progress. Jess was given the *CORE Phoneme Segmentation Test, the CORE Phonics Survey Reading and Decoding Record Form* and various short passages at a third-grade level. The assessments used for the math interventions were timed fact family sheets and teacher-made sheets for reading and writing numbers to the millions' place.

Action Step 5: Monitor Progress

After completing the Response to Intervention Plan Summary, we set up the charts and graphs in an Excel spreadsheet. The goal, ART, and the dates of the assessments were entered. The diagnostic assessment was used to establish a baseline for the data, and it was entered into the graph before beginning the interventions.

This is the way the graphs looked at the beginning of the intervention period. The only score was the baseline. All the baseline graphs will look this way at the beginning.

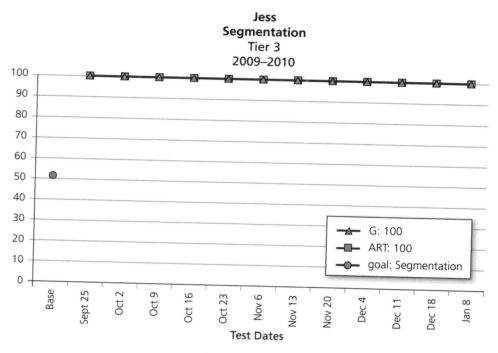

Figure 48

Dates	G 100	ART 100	goal Segmentation	G	ART	goal Phonics	G	ART	goal Comprehension-3rd
Base			52	100	100	68	100	80	40
Test Dates									
Sept 25	100	100	72	100	100	98	100	80	40
Oct 2	100	100	87	100	100	95	100	80	50
Oct 9	100	100	80	100	100	93	100	80	80
Oct 16	100	100	93	100	100	80	100	80	55
Oct 23	100	100	93	100	100	91	100	80	80
Nov 6	100	100	93	100	100	93	100	80	42
Nov 13	100	100	100	100	100	100	100	80	80
Nov 20	100	100	100	100	100	100	100	80	71
Dec 4	100	100	100	100	100	100	100	80	80
Dec 11	100	100		100	100		100	80	50
Dec 18	100	100		100	100		100	80	100
Jan 8	100	100		100	100		100	80	28

Figure 49: (For a blank table, see the Tracking Table form in the Appendix on page 100.)

Each week, a score was entered in the **reading** table so a new data point would be displayed on the Tier 3 graph.

	G	ART	goal 1	G	ART	goal 2	G	ART	goal 3
Dates	12	12	add/sub facts	100	80	Reading No.s	100	100	Writing No.s
Base			2			60			100
Test Dates									
Sept 25	12	12	2	100	80	60	100	100	0
Oct 2	12	12	2	100	80	80	100	100	100
Oct 9	12	12	2	100	80	80	100	100	80
Oct 16	12	12	3	100	80	80	100	100	100
Oct 23	12	12	4	100	80	100	100	100	60
Nov 6	12	12	4	100	80	80	100	100	100
Nov 13	12	12	4	100	80	100	100	100	100
Nov 20	12	12	5	100	80	100	100	100	100
Dec 4	12	12	5	100	80	100	100	100	100
Dec 18	12	12	5	100	80		100	100	

Figure 50

Each week, a score was entered in the **math** table so a new data point would be displayed on the Tier 3 graph.

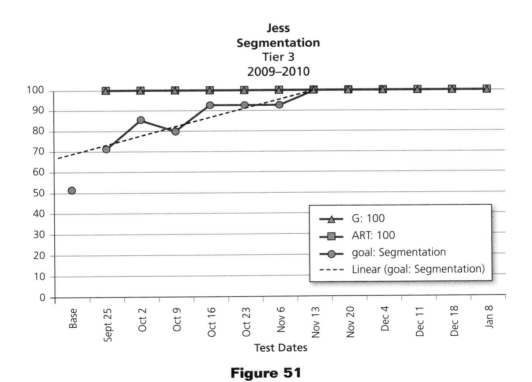

Figure 51

The results from this Tier 3 intervention showed that in the seventh, eighth, and ninth weeks, Jess achieved her goal of 100 percent on segmentation.

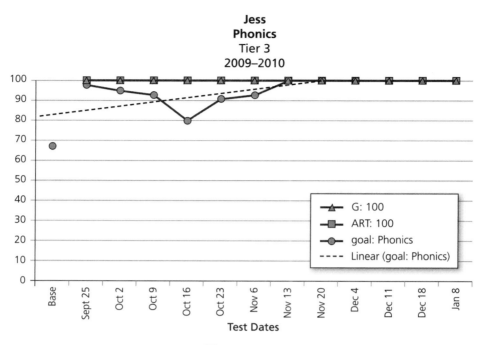

Figure 52

The results from this Tier 3 intervention showed that in the seventh, eighth, and ninth weeks, Jess achieved her goal of 100 percent on phonics.

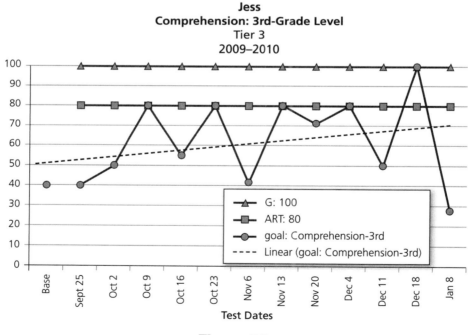

Figure 53

The results from this Tier 3 intervention showed that Jess scored between the ART and the goal only one time.

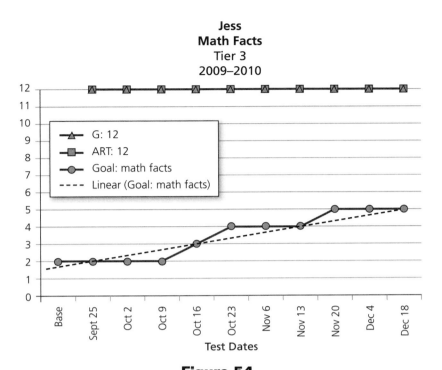

Figure 54

The results from this Tier 3 intervention showed that Jess scored significantly below the ART and the goal.

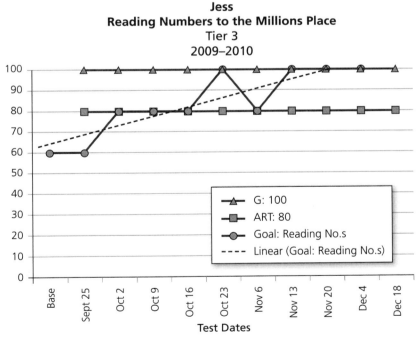

Figure 55

The results from this Tier 3 intervention showed that Jess reached her goal in the fifth, seventh, eighth, and ninth weeks with 100 percent accuracy.

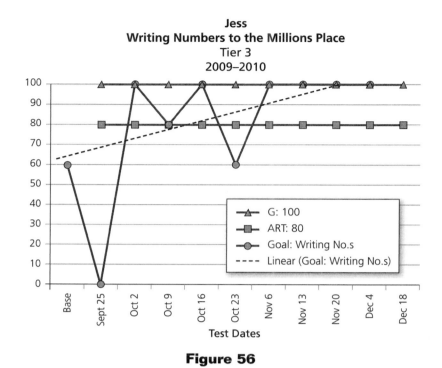

Figure 56

The results from this Tier 3 intervention showed that Jess reached her goal in the second, fourth, sixth, seventh, eighth, and ninth weeks.

Each week a score was entered in the reading table, so a new data point would be displayed on the Tier 2 graph.

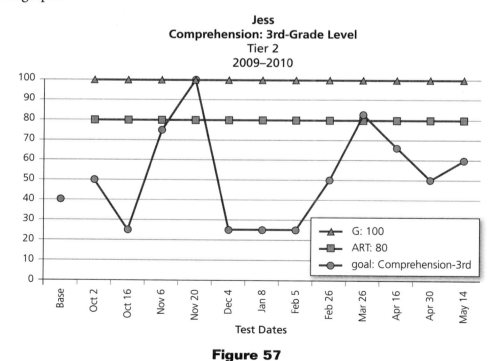

Figure 57

	G	ART	goal
Dates	100	80	**Comprehension-third**
Base			40
Test Dates			
Oct 2	100	80	50
Oct 16	100	80	25
Nov 6	100	80	75
Nov 20	100	80	100
Dec 4	100	80	25
Jan 8	100	80	25
Feb 5	100	80	25
Feb 26	100	80	50
Mar 26	100	80	83
Apr 16	100	80	67
Apr 30	100	80	50
May 14	100	80	60

Figure 58

The results from this Tier 2 intervention showed minimal progress in Jess' acquisition of comprehension strategies and were less successful than the Tier 3 comprehension intervention.

Action Step 6: Analyze Data and Determine Possible Outcomes

Jess' progress was reviewed by the intervention team at the sixth and twelfth weeks. At the sixth week, the team noted the reading progress in segmentation and phonics but continued the intervention until Jess reached her goal three times in a row. It noted the lack of consistent progress in comprehension and decided to continue the intervention with increased intensity.

The team also noted the slow progress in the math-facts goal and decided to intensify the intervention. It noted the promising progress in reading and writing numbers to the millions' place. The team continued the Tier 2 interventions and increased the intensity there as well.

By the twelfth week, the intervention team decided to remove Jess from segmentation and phonics Tier 3 interventions, but decided to continue the comprehension interventions. Although she had not been successful, Jess needed the support. The team decided to change Jess' Tier 3 math facts intervention to a Tier 2 intervention due to the slow progress. They felt she could be just as successful receiving this intervention at the Tier 2 level. They decided to remove Jess from the reading and writing numbers interventions.

At the completion of the school year, Jess' Nevada Criterion-Referenced Test (CRT) result in English language arts was 228 and her Math score was 242. (A score of 300 is considered proficient.) Although she had made significant progress, she was still not proficient. Her school district survey assessment in English language arts was 43 percent and her math was 40 percent. Jess' interventions were helping her with individual skills but not with comprehension. This was preventing her from bridging the achievement gap.

Due to her lack of progress and response to the interventions, the team decided to refer Jess to our Multiple Disciplinary Team for evaluation for possible special-education services. Jess was evaluated before the end of her fourth-grade year and qualified for special-education services.

ADDITIONAL RESOURCES

— APPENDIX —

Blank Forms & Templates

If you would like to digitally download all the forms and templates found in this book for customization purposes, please visit Maupin House Publishing's website:

www.maupinhouse.com/practical-guide-to-rti.html
Scroll down to "Free Downloads" and click "Blank Forms & Templates."

PARENT NOTIFICATION LETTER

Date: _____

To the Parents/Guardian of: _____

Dear _____,

As we have discussed, your child is experiencing some difficulties in school. In an effort to help him/her succeed in my classroom, I am working with our school's Intervention Team to identify solutions to these difficulties. Team members include classroom teachers, the RTI Facilitator, the school psychologist and the principal.

Enclosed is a Confidential Family History form. Please complete the form and return it to me as soon as possible. This form will provide background information that may be helpful in understanding your child's difficulties and developing a classroom intervention plan that will help him/her be more successful in school. As the intervention plan is implemented, I will keep you informed regarding your child's progress.

Thank you for your assistance. With your help and support, I can better meet your child's needs. If you have any questions, please feel free to contact me at _____.

Sincerely,

Classroom Teacher

RESPONSE TO INTERVENTION   Confidential Family History

Date: _____ Student: _____

ID Number: _____ BD: _____ Age: _____

School: _____ Teacher: _____ Grade: _____

Parents: _____ Phone Numbers: _____

Student Health History

Concerns	Yes	No	Description of Concern
Infant			
Current			
Hearing			
Vision			
Dental			
Crawling			
Walking			
Speaking			

Check all that apply

My child

___ attended pre-school

___ attended Kindergarten

___ was retained

___ has learning problems

___ has trouble completing homework

___ has language problems

___ likes school

___ makes friends easily

___ gets mad easily

___ gets frustrated often

___ has frequent mood changes

___ is sad or cries often

___ is cooperative

Our Family

___ has experienced separation or divorce

___ has experienced family illness

___ has experienced death

___ There were medical problems during pregnancy

___ There were complications during birth

Other: _____

_____

_____

_____

_____

RESPONSE TO INTERVENTION

School Records Review

Date: _____ Student: _____ ID Number: _____ BD: _____ Age: _____

School: _____ Teacher: _____ Grade: _____

Student Educational History

Concerns	Yes	No	Description of Concern

Attendance Problem			Days absent/present
			   Current year _____/_____
			   Prior year _____/_____

Behavioral Problems			
Health Issues			
ELL			
Remedial Programs			
Retained			
Special Education			
Transiency			Name all schools

Parental Notification

Date	Phone	Conference	Progress Reports	Unsatisfactory Notices	Report Card

Other: _____

_____

_____

_____

_____

_____

_____

_____

INTERVENTION TEAM MEETING AGENDA

CORE screenings completed:

Students receiving Tier 2 interventions
Added:

Exited:

Students receiving Tier 3 interventions
Added:

Exited:

Proposals for 5th Grade

Concerns:

Follow Ups:

Psychologist Testing List
MDT Referrals

TIERED INSTRUCTION LIST

Last Name	First Name	Tier 1	Tier 2 (Small Grp Instruction)	Tier 3 (2:1 or 1:1 Instruction)

RESPONSE TO INTERVENTION

TIER 3

Plan Summary

Date: _____ Student: _____ ID Number: _____ BD: _____ Age: _____

School: _____ Teacher: _____ Grade: _____

Educational Concerns:	Type of Measurement:

Targeted Skills:

1.

2.

3.

Baseline

Skill 1	Skill 2	Skill 3

Goals (Specific statement of expected results of the intervention and the condition under which the student will perform the behavior)

1.

2.

3.

Target Goal and ART	Goal	ART
Skill 1		
Skill 2		
Skill 3		

Resources:		
Person Responsible:		

Start Date:		End Date:	

Number of Instructional Sessions	Skill 1	Skill 2	Skill 3
Minutes per Session			

TRACKING TABLE

	G	ART		G	ART		G	ART	
Dates									
Base									
Base									
Test Dates									

Universal Screening, Diagnostic Assessments, and Progress-Monitoring Sources

AIMSweb (www.aimsweb.com) is a benchmark and progress-monitoring system based on direct, frequent, and continuous student assessment.

Center on Instruction (www.centeroninstruction.org) has a collection of scientifically based resources on instruction.

The Consortium on Reading Excellence (CORE) (www.corelearn.com) provides technical assistance, professional development, and a variety of educational materials to schools as well as state departments of education.

The Dynamic Indicators of Basic Early Literacy Skills (DIBELS) (http://dibels.uoregon.edu) promotes using data from Curriculum-Based Measurements to make instructional decisions for students.

easyCBM (www.easycbm.com) was developed by the University of Oregon to be a district-level assessment system for RTI that includes benchmarking, progress-monitoring and comprehensive reporting.

Edcheckup (www.edcheckup.com) offers generic assessments to progress-monitor students and identify students who are at risk.

Hasbrouck-Tindal Table of Oral Reading Fluency Norms (www.readnaturally.com/howto/whoneeds.htm) is a company that develops and supports reading programs that support the five components of reading. Replace with something like: shows oral reading fluency rates of students in grades one through eight, allowing teachers to draw conclusions and make decisions about the oral reading fluency of their students.

IDEA Partnership Grant (www.ideapartnership.org) The IDEA Partnership is a group of more than fifty national organizations that works to improve educational outcomes for students with disabilities.

Intervention Central (www.interventioncentral.org) provides free resources to assist with implementing RTI and help struggling learners be successful.

IRIS Center for Training Enhancement (http://iris.peabody.vanderbilt.edu/onlinemodules.html) provides teacher resources on a variety of educational subjects through modules, case studies, activities, and podcasts.

National Center on Student Progress Monitoring (www.studentprogress.org) provides information, tools and resources on progress monitoring for teachers and parents.

Research Institute on Progress Monitoring (www.progressmonitoring.net) developed a progress-monitoring system to evaluate the results of individual instruction in the general education setting.

Renaissance Learning (www.renlearn.com) provides technology based programs for school improvement and student assessments.

RTI Action Network (www.rtinetwork.org) is dedicated to RTI and its implementation, so all students may receive appropriate instruction.

Sopris West (www.sopriswest.com) provides educational materials and professional development on a variety of educational topics.

System to Enhance Educational Performance (STEEP) (www.isteep.com) develops practices and materials with scientific merit and assists schools with implementation.

Yearly ProgressPro (www.mhdigitallearning.com) develops a variety of assessments and reports to support schools.

Intervention Websites and Resources

The Access Center (www.k8accesscenter.org) provides technical assistance that strengthens both state and local capacity to help students with disabilities effectively learn in the general education curriculum.

Council for Exceptional Children (www.cec.sped.org) is an organization dedicated to improving the educational success of individuals with disabilities and/or gifts and talents.

EverythingESL (www.everythingesl.net) provides lesson plans, teaching tips, and resources for educators working with English-language learners.

The Florida Center for Reading Research (www.fcrr.org) conducts research, disseminates information, and provides technical assistance in research based practices in reading instruction.

International Reading Association (www.reading.org) is the official site for IRA members and provides resources and information for literacy professionals.

Learning Disabilities Association of America (www.ldanatl.org) serves members with learning disabilities, their families, and the professionals who work with them by advocating for individuals with learning disabilities.

Learning First Alliance (www.learningfirst.org) is a partnership of sixteen education associations dedicated to improving student learning in America's public schools.

Learning-Focused (www.learningfocused.com) provides services, professional development, resources, products, technology support, and consultants to assist with increasing student performance.

National Association of School Psychologists (www.nasponline.org) NASP represents school psychology and supports school psychologists to enhance the learning and mental health of all children and youth.

National Association of State Directors of Special Education (www.nasdse.org) provides leadership focused on the improvement of educational services and positive outcomes for children and youth with disabilities throughout the United States, the federal territories and the Freely Associated States of Palau, Micronesia, and the Marshall Islands.

National Center for Learning Disabilities (www.ld.org) is an organization that works to ensure success for all individuals with learning disabilities in school, at work, and in life.

National Center on Response to Intervention (www.rti4success.org) provides information, resources, communication, and state resources on implementation of RTI.

National Council of Teachers of Mathematics (www.nctm.org) is a public voice of mathematics education supporting teachers to ensure equitable mathematics learning of the highest quality for all students through vision, leadership, professional development, and research.

National Center for the Dissemination of Disability Research (www.ncddr.org) focuses on knowledge translation of NIDRR-sponsored research and development results into evidence-based instruments and systematic reviews.

National Council for Teachers of English (www.ncte.org) is devoted to improving the teaching and learning of English and the language arts at all levels of education.

National Reading Panel (www.nationalreadingpanel.org) is a partnership with the National Institute for Literacy (NIFL) and the U.S. Department of Education (ED) to work on continued dissemination and implementation efforts of the NRP Report, as part of NIFL's overall mission to disseminate and implement research-based reading practices.

Peer-Assisted Learning Strategies (http://kc.vanderbilt.edu/pals) is a version of class-wide peer tutoring that combines proven instructional principles and practices and peer mediation so that research-based reading and math activities are effective, feasible, and enjoyable.

Solution Tree (www.solution-tree.com) connects practitioners with authors and other practitioners to address the challenges faced by educators today.

The What Works Clearinghouse (http://ies.ed.gov/ncee/wwc) reviews the vast amounts of research and provides educators with the information they need to make evidence-based decisions.

GLOSSARY
OF TERMS

Acceptable Response Threshold (ART): The Acceptable Response Threshold is the least amount of progress a student can make while still closing the achievement gap.

Achievable goals: Achievable goals are goals which are reasonable for an average student to achieve.

Ambitious goals: Ambitious goals are goals that are set high enough, yet achievable in order to close the achievement gap.

Assessment for learning: Assessment for learning is assessment that is used to guide instruction.

Case manager: A case manager is a representative for each grade level or department who acts as a liaison for the rest of the grade level or department.

Criterion Referenced Test (CRT): A Criterion Referenced Test is a test that is based on a set of criterion/standards that students are measured against.

Curriculum-Based Assessments (CBA): A Curriculum-Based Assessment is an informal measurement that could be created by teachers to determine a student's level of proficiency and is used to make instructional decisions.

Curriculum-Based Measurement (CBM): A Curriculum-Based Measurement is a formal measurement used to screen and/or monitor a student's progress in basic academic areas like reading, writing, and math.

Cut score or threshold: A cut score or threshold is a minimal level of performance that indicates if a student is performing at a proficient level.

Diagnostic Assessment: A diagnostic assessment is a method of determining a student's specific skill deficits and is used to determine intervention levels.

Differentiated instruction: Differentiated instruction is instruction delivered in a way that helps students learn at varying levels. Areas that could be differentiated are content, process, and/or product.

Discrepancy model: A discrepancy model is a model that compares a student's ability level to their performance level and has traditionally been used to determine if a student has a specific learning disability.

Fidelity: Fidelity is when an intervention is implemented as it was intended.

Individuals with Disabilities Education Act: Individuals with Disabilities Education Act is a federal law that was originally enacted in 1975 to ensure that students with disabilities have the opportunity to receive a free appropriate public education.

Individuals with Disabilities Education Improvement Act (IDEIA): Individuals with Disabilities Education Improvement Act is the reauthorization of IDEA in 2004 which allowed schools to use scientifically based research interventions as part of the evaluation process.

Intervention: An intervention is instruction that is specifically designed to address a skill deficit a student might have, and may be delivered at various levels of intensity in addition to the regular instruction delivered in Tier 1.

Literacy: Literacy is the ability to read, write, speak and think critically.

Multi-Disciplinary Team: A Multi-Disciplinary Team is a team of professionals that reviews all data gathered on a student to determine if the student should be referred for special-education evaluation.

No Child Left Behind Act (NCLBA): This bill was passed in 2001 and addressed the concerns of children in public education. The bill required students be proficient in reading and math by 2013–2014. Schools are required to give annual standardized assessments and demonstrate annual yearly progress.

Norm Referenced Test: A Norm Referenced Test is a test that determines the ranking of a student's ability in comparison to a particular group on a standardized assessment.

Numeracy: Numeracy is the ability to reason with numbers.

Paraprofessionals: Paraprofessionals are nonlicensed instructional assistants.

Problem-Solving Model: A Problem-Solving Model is a model that creates highly individualized instruction for each student based on their need.

Progress-monitoring: Progress-monitoring is data that is gathered on a regularly scheduled basis that is used to determine progress towards interventions that are given.

Professional Learning Community: A Professional Learning Community is a group of administrators, teachers, paraprofessionals, parents and students working together to ensure the best learning environment and instruction for all students.

Research-Based Interventions: Research-Based Interventions are interventions that have been proven to be effective through valid research studies.

Response to Intervention (RTI): Response to Intervention is a process to determine how a student responds to instruction when an intervention is administered.

Standard Treatment Protocol: A Standard Treatment Protocol uses pre-established intervention programs that deliver the same instruction to all students that receive them.

Structured Teacher Planning Time: Structured Teacher Planning Time is a meeting with teachers and administrators to analyze the results of common assessments and align expectations.

Supplemental Instruction: Supplemental Instruction is anything that is given in addition to the core instruction.

Team-based problem solving: Team-based problem solving is a diverse group of professionals reviewing data to make educational decisions about a student.

Universal Screening Tool: A Universal Screening Tool is an assessment tool usually administered 3 times a year to screen all students and help identify which students may need additional support to be successful.

Watch List: A Watch List identifies students who are not being successful in Tier 1 and would benefit from support in Tier 2 or Tier 3 instruction.

BIBLIOGRAPHY

1. Consortium on Reading Excellence, Inc. (CORE), *Assessing Reading, Multiple Measures for Kindergarten through Eighth Grade*, Novato, CA: Academic Therapy Pubns, 1999.

2. Deno, "Curriculum-Based Measurement: The Emerging Alternative," *Exceptional Children* 52(3) (1985): 219–232.

3. Dufour and Eaker, *Professional Learning Communities at Work, Best Practices for Enhancing Student Achievement*. Bloomington, IN: National Educational Service, 1998.

4. Fuchs, Fuchs, Hamlett, Phillips, and Bentz, "Classwide Curriculum-Based Measurement: Helping General Educators Meet the Challenge of Student Diversity," *Exceptional Children*, 60(6) (1994):518–537.

5. Gersten, Beckmann, Clarke, Foegen, Marsh, Star, and Witzel, "Assisting students struggling with mathematics: Response to Intervention (RTI) for elementary and middle schools" (NCEE 2009–4060), *Washington, DC: National Center for Education Evaluation and Regional Assistance, Institute of Education Sciences, U.S. Department of Education.* Retrieved from http://ies.ed.gov/ncee/wwc/publications/practiceguides/ (2009).

6. Gersten, R., Compton, D., Connor, C.M., Dimino, J., Santoro, L., Linan-Thompson,S., and Tilly, W.D. (2008). *Assisting Students Struggling with Reading: Response to Intervention and Multi-tier Intervention for Reading in the Primary Grades. A Practice Guide.* (NCEE 2009–4045). Washington, DC: National Center for Education Evaluation and Regional Assistance, Institute of Education Sciences, U.S. Department of Education. Retrieved from http://ies.ed.gov/ncee/wwc/publications/practiceguides/.

7. Gersten, Clarke, and Jordan, "Screening for Mathematics Difficulties in K-3 students," Portsmouth, HN: RMC Research Corporation, Center on Instruction, 2007.

8. Shinn and Bamonto, "Advanced applications of curriculum-based measurement: "Big ideas" and avoiding confusion," In M. R. Shinn. (Ed.) *Advanced Applications of Curriculum-Based Measurement*. New York, NY: The Guilford Press, 1998.

9. Stiggins, Arter, Chappuis, and Chappuis, *Classroom Assessment for Student Learning, Doing it Right-Using it Well*. Portland, OR: Assessment Training Institute, Inc., 2004.

10. The University of Texas System/Texas Education Agency, *Introduction to the 3-Tier Reading Model: Reducing Reading Difficulties for Kindergarten through Third Grade Students (Third Edition)*. Austin TX: University of Texas at Austin, College of Education, 2005.

11. Vadasy, Sanders, and Tudor, "Effectiveness of Paraeducator-Supplemented Individual Instruction: Beyond Basic Decoding Skills," *Journal of Learning Disabilities*, 40(6), (2007): 508–525.